LEARNING TO BE STRONG

*Setting up a neighbourhood service
for under-fives and their families*

LEARNING TO BE STRONG

*Setting up a neighbourhood service
for under-fives and their families*

MARGY WHALLEY

SERIES EDITOR TINA BRUCE

Hodder & Stoughton

A MEMBER OF THE HODDER HEADLINE GROUP

Cataloguing in Publication Data is available from the British Library

ISBN 0 340 57631 6

First published 1994

Impression number   10 9 8 7 6 5 4 3 2 1
Year   1998 1997 1996 1995 1994

Typeset by Wearset, Boldon, Tyne and Wear
Printed in Great Britain for Hodder & Stoughton Educational, a division of Hodder Headline Plc, Mill Road, Dunton Green, Sevenoaks, Kent TN13 2YA by Thomson Litho Ltd, East Kilbride.

This book is dedicated to my daughter Tasha who has grown at least six inches while I have been writing it and who has kept me going with her love and sense of humour.

ACKNOWLEDGMENTS

I'd like firstly to thank my parents, Richard and Mary Whalley, who encouraged me to ask questions when I didn't understand and to challenge when I didn't agree. I would also like to thank my friends, Rosie Bose and Meryal Orr for being so nurturing and for their many hours of practical support. I want to express my gratitude to Katey Mairs, Tina Bruce, Carol Ashford and Faye Page: strong, powerful and intelligent women colleagues who helped me to find enough confidence in myself to write this book.

I'd like to thank John Welsh who taught me so much about working in the community, Geoff Marshall who encouraged me to take risks and make mistakes when I was a probationary teacher twenty years ago, and councillor Jimmy Kane who has given me a great deal of moral support since I came to work in Corby. I want to thank *all* the staff at Pen Green, past and present, and particularly Trevor Chandler for being so consistently caring. Mary Champion and Di Brewster at Pen Green deserve special thanks for deciphering my handwriting; and thanks to Paula Thompson at Montsaye School for typing – often into the small hours. Thanks also to Anne Robinson at the National Children's Bureau and Dr Peter Whalley at the Open University for help with books and references, and to Alaide Santos for her insight into what was important at Pen Green.

I would also like to thank the following for the right to use their photographs: British Steel Heritage Centre at East Carlton Park, Corby; Ellen Neal, Jean Heywood, Robert Orr and Tom Maxwell.

Finally, I'd like to thank all the parents and children who have been and still are very important to me.

The ideas expressed in this book are the author's own and do not necessarily reflect those of the Northamptonshire County Council.

CONTENTS

Series Preface – 0–8 Years: The First Phase of Living

At most times in history and in most parts of the world, the first eight years of life have been seen as the first phase of living. Ideally, during this period, children learn who they are; about those who are significant to them; and how their world is. They learn to take part, and how to contribute creatively, imaginatively, sensitively and reflectively.

Children learn through and with the people they love and the people who care for them. They learn through being physically active, through real, direct experiences, and through learning how to make and use symbolic systems, such as play, language and representation. Whether children are at home, in nursery schools, classes, family centres, day nurseries, or playgroups, workplace nurseries, primary schools or whatever, they need informed adults who can help them. The series will help those who work with young children, in whatever capacity, to be as informed as possible about this first phase of living.

From the age of eight years all the developing and learning can be consolidated, hopefully in ways which build on what has gone before.

In this series, different books emphasise different aspects of the first phase of living. *Getting to Know You* and *Learning to be Strong* give high status to adults (parents and early-childhood specialists of all kinds) who love and work with children. *Getting to Know You*, by Lynne Bartholomew and Tina Bruce focuses on the importance of adults in the lives of children. Observing children in spontaneous situations at Redford House Nursery (a workplace nursery) and in a variety of other settings, the book emulates the spirit of Susan Isaacs. This means using theory to interpret observations and recording the progress of children as they are supported and extended in their development and learning. The book is full of examples of good practice in record-keeping. Unless we know and understand our children, unless we act effectively on what we know, we cannot help them very much.

Learning to be Strong, by Margy Whalley, helps us to see how important it is that all the adults living with or working with children act as a team. This is undoubtedly one of the most important kinds of partnership that human beings ever make. When adults come together and use their energy in an orchestrated way on behalf of the child, then quality and excellent progress are seen. Pen Green Centre for Under-fives and Families is the story of the development of a kind of partnership which Margaret McMillan would have admired. Beacons of excellence continue to shine and illuminate practice through the ages, transcending the passing of time.

Just as the first two books emphasise the importance of the adult helping the child, the next two focus *on* the child. John Matthews helps us to focus on one of the ways in which children learn to use symbolic systems. In *Representation in Childhood*, he looks at how children keep hold of the experiences they have through the process of representation. Children's drawings and paintings are looked at in a way which goes beyond the superficial, and help us to understand details. This means the adult can help the child better. Doing this is a complex process, but the book suggests ways which are easy to understand and is full of real examples.

Later in the series, Mollie Davies looks at *Movement* (which includes dance) and its major contributions to development and learning. She focuses on actions, as well as representations, play and language, demonstrating that movement is truly one of the basics. She gives many practical examples to help those working with children enjoy movement with confidence, bringing together actions, feelings, thoughts and relationships.

Other books in the series will underline the importance of adults working together to become informed in order to help children develop and learn.

Clinging to dogma, 'I believe children need . . .' or saying 'What was good enough for me . . .' is not good enough. Children deserve better than that. The pursuit of excellence means being informed. This series will help adults increase their knowledge and understanding of the 'first phase of living', and to act in the light of this for the good of children.

TINA BRUCE

INTRODUCTION

I was told that writing a book was going to be like giving birth. For me it's been more like giving blood. I've never stopped feeling afraid that I wouldn't find the words to do justice to the energy, compassion and creativity of the many colleagues with whom I have worked. The books that I have got most out of have always been the ones where writers seemed to believe in something very passionately. I have tried to hold on to my passion and give it a voice. I have always been fascinated by 'the things that don't fit' (Feynman, 1990) and in more than twenty years of working with children and families it is the angry child or the alienated adult who has interested me the most. I enjoy working where there's something to fight for or something to fight against and what has most impressed me about working in Corby for the last ten years, has been the strength and the warmth of a community where many have had to face unemployment and hardship.

I hope that what follows is an accurate representation of how parents, staff and children worked together to set up a Neighbourhood Centre for under-fives and families, a centre where people chose what kind of public services were most important to them and influenced how those services were delivered.

Each chapter demonstrates my commitment to integrated multi-disciplinary community-based services for families and to services that can be owned by the people using them.

> There is something very fine and developed in the centre's culture: a belief that parents and children know what they need and therefore what they want to do is very much respected. They have the opportunity to choose what is appropriate for themselves.
> (Santos, 1992)

1 PEN GREEN, A HISTORICAL PERSPECTIVE

PUTTING PEN GREEN IN CONTEXT: A COMMUNITY IN CORBY MAKES ITSELF HEARD

The history of the development of education and day-care services for young children reads like another kind of Hundred Years War with combatants representing conflicting ideologies of motherhood, different psychological theories of child development and different political agendas. Sometimes services for children have expanded substantially. Sometimes they have been frozen or cut back. Rarely has there been any regard for the views of parents or the children themselves.

Pen Green is the story of how a service for under-fives and their families developed in one community, in Corby, Northamptonshire. It is principally the story of how women and children carved out from granite-like bureaucratic structures a service which met *their* needs and also honoured those of young children by celebrating their existence. This service enabled women to take time to work, time to care and time for themselves (Ghedini, 1990) and supported families, however they were constituted, within their own community.

Men are important in this story; without the generosity and support of local politicians (predominantly male) and the men who have worked in the centre it would have been impossible at times to move things forward. Fathers are increasingly involved in caring, educating and planning for their own children within the nursery, and are finding support for themselves within the centre. (For an account of a man working in a child-care setting see Chandler in Rouse 1990, and Chandler 1993.)

It is not the aim of this chapter to give a historical account of how provision for under-fives and their families developed in Britain but it is important to put what happened in Corby in to some kind of context. The three consistent policy strands which Gillian Pugh (1987, p. 301) identifies as present in the development of education and care services for children in this country, certainly influenced developments in Corby. These strands are concerned with: children's developmental needs; the needs of families for support; and equal opportunities for women aided by the provision of adequate day-care facilities.

The impact of local politics

Without statutory requirement to provide services for children under five at a national level, developments in Corby were very much influenced by, and vulnerable to, whichever administration was in office (Blackstone, 1973). When there was a strong alliance between the chair of the education and social services committees and when members and officers in the relevant departments had a commitment to offering integrated day-care and education provision for young children, radical changes were effected.

It would be wrong to underplay the degree to which local, county, and national politics have influenced the development of the centre.

When in 1975 a report reviewed the provision for under-fives in Northamptonshire, in educational terms it reflected the compensatory viewpoint of the sixties and early seventies. While acknowledging the needs of all under-fives it stated that services would have to be geared to children with 'particular problems'. From a social services viewpoint, it emphasised the preventative, and child protection aspects of pre-fives' services. The report clearly stated that the only way forward was to set up experimental provision jointly planned, managed and financed by Education and Social Services Departments and other interested departments and agencies.

The report, referring to flexible 'hybrid' under-fives' centres in the London authorities and to the operational difficulties experienced in setting up such centres, recommended that two experimental projects should be set up in the county in areas of social need. These would offer a wider provision than either traditional nursery education or day-care.

The agencies work together

From 1977 to 1981 the projects were put on hold. However, in December 1981 new discussions on joint services for the under-fives took place between social services, the Education Department and the Health Authority. By March 1982 the decision was made: a Corby Under-Fives' Centre should be set up with a single multi-disciplinary team under one manager. All staff were to have the same conditions of service. Funding for the project was initially to be by joint financing through the Joint Consultative Committee of the County Council and the Area Health Authority.

Scarce resources for young children and families

Northamptonshire was grappling with problems that were being experienced nationally. Despite Plowden (1967), Halsey (1972), and the Urban Programme, nursery education was *still* only reaching twenty per cent of three-year-olds in England. (Parry and Archer, 1974; Riley, 1983).

Government rhetoric implied nursery education would be made generally available (DES, Education: A framework for Expansion, 1972) but a 'compensatory model' of nursery provision prevailed. Parents (mothers) were to be encouraged to attend and receive 'expert guidance' in the education of their children. Day care had become 'a scarce resource to be allocated by social workers to demoralised parents' (Penn, 1984) and parents had to become 'clients' in order to receive what services were available.

The multi-agency steering group that was set up to make plans for the new Corby centre steered an uneasy course through these troubled waters. The chart on page 4 shows our interpretation of the kind of belief systems and practice in operation during the seventies and eighties within the education and social services departments. It also shows where the proposed new centre fitted in.

Groundwork: the impact of community social workers

In April 1982 in Northampton, a community social worker carried out a comprehensive data review and questionnaire, had discussions with professional workers and made visits with professional colleagues to other centres of interest. At the same time in Corby, the community social worker worked with and listened to local families and helped set up a community action group. This group immediately requested representation on the staff appointments panel at the proposed new Pen Green Centre. The structural relationship between staff and parents at Pen Green was determined by the need for staff to be immediately accountable to a strong and vocal consumer group. This led to a partnership that was 'equal but different' between workers in, and users of, the services.

> Parents who are not defined as 'inept' and who are not competing for a scarce resource are less likely to be passively grateful and deferential and to want to determine the nature of the service provided for their children.
> (Haddock, 1981)

Learning to be strong

> Education, and probably early childhood education more than any other area, is political. It is about the distribution of power, the exertion of influence and the

	Existing social services day nurseries/child protection model	Existing education nursery units/compensatory nursery education model	New proposal: Education and Care Community-Based Integrated Approach (e.g. Pen Green)
Management	Mechanistic/hierarchical. Supervisory structure in place but not effective	Mechanistic/hierarchical. No supervisory structure. Nursery units have relatively little autonomy	Staff work co-operatively with a clear management structure. All staff have supervision. Major emphasis on user control, power sharing
Staff attitude	Focus on caring for the young child. More recently 'parenting the parent'	Focus on 'educating' role with the pre-school child. Professional model	Complementary expertise. Parents/'clients' can be service providers. Education and care equally important
Beliefs about parent(s)	Beliefs about abusive, neglecting mothers. Existence of, and role of, fathers rarely addressed	Inadequate parenting – lack of stimulation for child	Commitment to equal opportunities. Women's right to work recognised and parent's right to be involved in the education and care of their child
Parents 'role'	Policing and parent education	Parents to learn from the school: rhetoric of 'parent/professional partnership'	Parents are very interested in their own child's development and education. Parent = child's first educator, parents have rights, must be consulted
Beliefs about the needs of children	Child protection; a focus on children at risk or failing to thrive. Focus on *caring* for the child	Concerned with children's emotional and developmental needs. Providing a 'universal' service but also targeting children with specific difficulties	Children's right to be educated and cared for in their own community. Recognition that stereotypes aren't useful. Address the needs of children as individuals
Pedagogy – how we are teaching the children, how children learn, how their learning develops and how we extend their play	Didactic and/or behaviourist approach. Children are 'taught' the skills nursery nurses think are important	*Laissez faire* – teacher puts out 'creative play' activities and child plays freely. Alternatively a skills acquisition approach. Preparing children for infant school	Children have the right to choose. Interactionist – teachers match worth-while curriculum content to children's observed cognitive structures (Athey, 1990)
Quality assurance	Children Act 1989 and local authority appeals procedure	Education Act 1981, Education Reform Act, 1988. Parent's Charter. School governors	Accountability to parents' group/family group. Written policy documents compiled by staff and parents that can be verified. Explicit complaints procedure
Involvement with other agencies	Formal allocation meet-ings and case reviews. Often no direct link with social workers most concerned with children in the day nursery	By telephone or at case conferences	Collaborative, informal daily use of Centre, plus formal meetings with written agenda.
Historical roots	Late Victorian, child protection: children as victims of feckless parents	USA: *Headstart*; EPAs; Eric Midwinter; Halsey; Plowden Report (1967)	Margaret McMillan, Community Educators in the sixties and seventies. Radical Voluntary Sector initiatives; Holman/Community Social Work; Workers Education Association; Adult Education

Figure 1   *Our interpretation of the belief systems and practice operating within education and social services departments in the seventies and eighties*

ability to provide people with the means to conserve and transform society.
(Chris Pascal, 1992)

This link between nursery education and politics has been honourably maintained over the ten years of the centre's history. Without the strong personal commitment and political awareness of the late Betty Lupton, then General Inspector for Primary Education in Northamptonshire, who nursed the project through its committee stages from 1976 to 1983 (a period which included three changes in administration) it is likely that the centre would have remained a paper exercise. Margaret McMillan had worked to the same end at the beginning of this century.

Margaret McMillan's motivation for advocating parental involvement was political . . . as a Christian Socialist she saw parent involvement as a way in which impoverished families could play a part in re-shaping their destinies and creating a new society. It was for this reason that she wanted parents to be accorded respect and even given control within the nurseries, helped to develop their ability, and encouraged to take part in political activity.
(Tizard, Mortimore and Burchell, 1981, p. 30)

Knowing your community

The word 'community' must be used advisedly. A community can be a few streets; a small group of people speaking one language, isolated in a hostile neighbourhood; a whole town or settlement supported by one industry, or a group of workers deprived of their livelihood, like the steelworkers in Corby. We are often given the impression that in the past communities were always warm, cosy and supportive, whereas Fletcher (1987) points out that 'The bonds could be of enmity'. Benington (1974) makes the point that politicians and professionals use the word community, 'as a kind of aerosol word to be sprayed on to deteriorating institutions to deodorise and humanise them.'
     We live in a society where social inequalities are increasing (Commission on Social Justice, 1993). A child's chance of survival may be five times greater than another's depending on his/her social class (Bradshaw, 1990), yet child mortality is said to be at an acceptable level. Services are often distributed without any real logic or fairness. Martin (1987) writes of communities whose experience is of 'endurance, resistance and struggle' and the Barclay Committee report (1982) refers to the 'shared experience of oppression'. This is

the kind of community which exists in Corby. In our curriculum document (1985) we wrote:

> *Whose Centre?*
> *Our children, parents and staff live and work in homes and buildings. These form streets. The streets are part of a community, which is East and West Lloyds and the Corby old village. This community has its own story and so does the Centre.*

Corby Town – 'Little Glasgow'

When children in Corby say that they are going 'up the road' it's not as straightforward a statement as it sounds. Buses run from Corby to Glasgow almost every day and many families living in Corby still have extended family links in Scotland. For these families the steelworks is not simply a legend and they may well have formed part of the immigrant work force which was attracted to the town in the thirties.

Corby was once a small village with a winding main street and pretty ironstone cottages. In 1880 it had a population of 611 people. By 1910 the first blast furnace had been built by the Lloyds Ironstone Company and the local population increased to 1,356. When Stewarts and Lloyds took over in 1923 Corby was chosen as the site for a new iron and steelworks and its huge workforce inevitably caused some problems locally. The directors of Stewarts and Lloyds had to provide living accommodation for more than 2,200 families. Corby was transformed from a rural agricultural community into a frontier steel town.

A housing estate for management and senior staff was established in beautiful parklands on the edge of the town.

> *. . . with the Park as a perfect playground for adults and children where you can wander amongst the magnificent trees, watch the deer browsing amongst the bracken and admire the spacious views across the valley of the River Welland in perfect content.*
> (*Estate Managers Handbook*, 1934)

After consultation with the workforce, the steelworkers' houses were built close to the works. Their homes were only separated by a railway and a sixty-foot strip of land from the blast furnaces.

Figure 2   Pen Green estate before 'the candle went out in Corby' with the closing of the steelworks

By the seventies Corby had become a 'mecca for employment', and had a population of more than 40,000. Migrant workers were given council houses within three weeks of the arrival of their family. Although Corby was advertised as 'a land of milk and honey', it was often regarded with suspicion and even hostility by residents of neighbouring towns and villages.

However, in March 1980 the British Steel Corporation closed the Iron and Steel Works. The 'Corby Candle' was a bleeder which burnt off excess gases produced during the steelmaking process and it was visible for miles around. When it finally went out, it marked the end of the steel working community.

Pen Green: one catchment area but three communities

From January to July 1983, staff at Pen Green got to know the local area which was made up of three distinct communities: the old Corby village; the houses which backed on to the steelworks; and the estate which linked them to the new town centre.

We were lucky that there were well-documented accounts of the area made by the social services team (Welsh, 1980). Social workers had many concerns in the early eighties about a local housing policy which had resulted in many 'families with problems' being placed on one estate. They described the area as a 'ghetto community of the elderly and the poor'. They also noted that there was a low uptake of existing welfare and support services. Local people seemed unwilling or unable to use what was on offer in the town centre. The community social workers advocated:

- free resources for children under five;

- adult education, but not of a formal nature;

- services for latch-key children;

- drop-in facilities for single parents and mothers at home;

- a localised health provision for young families.

Walking around our area in 1983 we saw houses boarded up and a row of shops barricaded with wire grills. Sulphur dioxide emissions from the blast furnaces had constantly bombarded the estate with yellow dust which eroded the brickwork and fittings. Because of this, windows were never opened in Pen Green Lane where the new centre was sited in the Samuel Lloyd comprehensive school. This thirties' school building was, and remains, the most distinctive and historic building in the new town. Older residents refer to it as 'the old clinic' because it was used as a health clinic during the war and more recently as a dental clinic. The old school site had housed adult basic education classes, discos for teenagers, playing fields and a swimming pool as well as mainstream provision for eleven to eighteen-year-olds. By 1983 however, it had been declared 'surplus to requirements' and local children attended comprehensive schools some distance from the estate.

Most of the children who would use the nursery lived in sub-standard, red-bricked steelworkers' 'cottages'. Throughout the 1980s these council houses were sold very cheaply to encourage new residents to buy. This gave the estate a very motley appearance. Boarded-up houses stood next to privately owned homes. There were few local facilities for women with children, although for men there were several unemployed workers' centres, as well as the British Steel Welfare Club, and a number of pubs.

Figure 3   The Pen Green Centre

The action group 'against' the centre

There were very few real voluntary groups in the estate but Pen Green staff made frequent visits to the local advisory group based at the community centre. Its members had actively campaigned to get representation on the steering group of the proposed new Pen Green Nursery and Family Centre, and had been involved in interviews for the senior staff. Local people viewed the advent of 'the new centre for problem families', as they saw it, as a threat to what had already been achieved for young people in the community, such as a youth group and a new and very vulnerable playgroup. They resented the fact that there had been no consultation between officers of the County Council setting up the new services and the people who were supposed to use them.

The Social Services Department

Until 1984 Corby worked a 'patch system' through which local social workers were in touch with community groups and local concerns. Corby then became part of the Corby/Kettering division and a 'referral and assessment team' and a 'long-term team' were set up. To the dismay of local social workers 'patch' and 'prevention' ceased to be words in common usage.

Health and poverty in Pen Green

Deprivation indicators such as the Jarman Index showed that the Pen Green area was one of the four most deprived areas in the county (1981 census). Poor nutrition, inadequate housing, high unemployment, and high infant mortality were all major factors influencing health care. Like social services, health-care services in Corby were centralised: brought in from local areas to the new prestigious health centres in the town centre. Parents were faced with a long walk or a long wait for public transport.

The value of time spent in reconnaissance and market research

By the time the centre officially opened on 4 July, 1983 we had:

- gathered a great deal of information about the community;

- listened and talked to representatives of local groups;

- read accounts of the area written by the local social work team;

- visited local playgroups and been inside local primary schools.

This meant that we could inform our decision-making and our practice with the views and expressed needs of local families. We could put into context all the good ideas which we saw in other centres (education, social services and voluntary sector provision) and make sure that these ideas were transferable to 'our patch'. We responded to ideas that professional colleagues identified as important and filled in the gaps which parents made us aware of, such as: responding to children with special needs during the holidays; offering children and their families a chance to get out and about in the minibus on day trips and residential holidays; providing adult community education services that were acceptable to local people; and by re-introducing localised health services inside the under-fives' centre. To have concentrated exclusively on setting up a quality nursery without this kind of knowledge of the community would have been a fundamental mistake.

2 FINDING A WAY THROUGH THE BUREAUCRACY – A COMMUNITY DEVELOPMENT APPROACH

A MULTI-DISCIPLINARY TEAM

In 1982 the Local Education Authority, the Local Authority Social Services Department and the Area Health Authority decided to jointly finance a community-based service for under-fives and their families. It was to be set up in a part of Corby which they had collectively identified as an area of need. Traditionally these three agencies offered highly differentiated services to families with young children. This time all the services were to be based on one site.

The service was to be staffed by a multi-disciplinary team led by a head of unit (a head teacher or principal social worker) appointed from either an education or social work background. Line management was to be the joint responsibility of the Education and Social Services Departments. By 1983 these were the two main funding bodies since the Area Health Authority was not in a position to fund running costs. Strategic policy making was the responsibility of a policy group (which took over the role of the original steering group) and was made up of officers from the Education and Social Services Departments at assistant director level; a clinical medical officer; a general inspector for primary education; parents and staff.

That such a high-powered group should direct the workings of a relatively small establishment was unusual and reflected a desire on the part of officers and members to move Northamptonshire's experimental under-fives' provision forward after seven years of committee-level and inter-departmental negotiation. With such high-powered 'ownership' of the work it was possible for the Pen Green staff group to work with the senior officers and challenge 'the fortified walls of local authorities' bureaucracies' (Fletcher, 1987).

All three departments (Health, Education and Social Services) had, throughout the sixties, seventies and eighties, placed an increased emphasis on the importance of user-participation (Plowden Report, 1967; Court Report, 1976; Barclay Report, 1982). They nominally espoused a 'partnership model' and emphasised the need for neighbourhood and community services which could be sensitive to the needs of families (Cumberlege Nursing Review, 1986). There was conflict, however, between rhetoric and practice. At a national level the history of services to young children and their families, 'professional jealousies' between the providers of services (Pugh, 1992) and the different priorities within each service (child protection, education, health care) made offering a coherent approach seem almost a practical impossibility.

The centre opened on 4 July 1983, at a time when government departments had at last acknowledged that families needed locally-based services: services not fragmented between government departments (Tomlinson, 1986; Pugh, 1992) and services which encouraged consumers to be actively involved in making decisions, rather than merely receiving welfare handouts (Holman, 1983). The centre survived a decade during which the partnership model in Education and Social Services, and the co-ordination of services at a local level, were consistently under legislative attack.

The new emphasis on the role of local authorities as *purchasers* of care from the private and voluntary sectors, rather than as *providers* of care, would seem to indicate a movement away from their being responsive to locally expressed need. As Pugh (1992) points out, The Children Act (1989) fails to accept that *all* children have a right to good quality, affordable services that will promote their all-round development, and the Act perpetuates the 'deficit-rescuing' model of providing care for our youngest children. The Education Reform Act (1988) and the Education (Schools) Act (1992) both substantially reduce the control of the local education authorities (Pugh, 1992; Elfer and Wedge, 1992) and make it even more difficult for the LEAs and the local authorities to co-operate to provide relevant, responsive local services to young families.

In setting up the centre we realised that it was essential to link not only with our three funding agencies, Education, Social Services and Health but also with the Housing Department, leisure services, the police, and the few existing voluntary organisations. We also needed to call on other sectors within our principal funding agencies, that were not primarily concerned with children's services, such as adult basic education, adult education, adult psychiatric services and the disability services. We realised that to provide an effective service it was inappropriate for us to separate the health education and social needs of children and families and that working co-operatively was cost-effective. The alternative was too confusing for families.

A RADICAL NEW APPROACH? CO-OPERATION BETWEEN AGENCIES, WORKERS AND PARENTS

The legislative changes of the late eighties and early nineties have made the jointly run services which we set up in Corby very vulnerable. We have, however, survived and maintained services at a very high level throughout the last ten years, despite the vagiaries of central and local government policy.

What we set up in 1983 was not an entirely new concept. After all, there was nothing new about putting a baby clinic next to a community nursery inside a family centre where day care was on offer. Margaret McMillan was working in this way in Deptford at the beginning of the century.

What was new, however, was that we set up a theoretical and management framework for the service and adopted a way of working which did not accept stereotypical views of parents, young children or nursery workers. It was a way of working that was based on co-operation between parents and workers: 'a radical notion of self-help as personal growth and the development of a sense of community responsibility' (Hevey, 1982).

Our thinking was influenced by Shirley Goodwin (1988), writing about the development of health-visiting:

> *The very principles of health-visiting are founded upon an acceptance of the professional responsibility to seek to challenge and influence public policy, rather than submissively assisting people to live with its consequences, taking all the blame themselves for their unhealthy lifestyles.*

We wanted to make services relevant, responsive and acceptable to local people. We knew that we would have to respond to new challenges, that we would need to work in an integrated way and that we needed to adopt inter-agency strategies.

Staffing policy at Pen Green: empowerment or policing?

Staff at the new Pen Green Centre needed to understand their roles and to understand the management structures of other departments and the constraints experienced by workers from other agencies in order to avoid a 'blaming' approach. To make it possible to work with difficult situations, staff also needed to know the community intimately and the issues faced by families in a decade which was marked by a substantial increase in poverty. The alternative was to become 'soft policemen', who were 'intervening in the family on behalf of the state' (Abbot, 1987). We knew, as professional workers, the fine line between empowerment and policing (Condry, 1986; Illich, 1977) and that humanising our job titles by calling ourselves 'family workers', instead of teachers or social workers, and using the phrase 'parent involvement' in our publicity material just wasn't enough.

What we wanted was to be part of a process outlined by students on an MA course in community education at the University of Leicester/Humberside:

- Community education should be concerned with the individual's capacity to be self directing.

- Community education should help individuals to gain more control over their lives.

- Community education should be about raising self-esteem.

- Community education should promote learning as a lifelong experience.

- Community education should be about equal opportunities.

- Community education should be about pushing boundaries.

- Community education should be about constructive discontent – not having to put up with things the way they are.

- Community education should encourage people to feel they have the power to change things.

- Community education should be about self-fulfilment.

The staff group at Pen Green needed to be clear about their values and power base. We did not want to be part of a service where all the power and control was retained by the workers. We wanted to relocate at least some of it back into the community. Giving back power, or more accurately, letting go of it, requires a willingness on the part of the professional worker to give up some control. Services needed to be more open, warm and accessible.

Staff also needed to accept that parents are not a homogeneous group (Atkin and Bastiani, 1987) and that there may well be no shared value base between groups of parents or between parents and some staff. (Staff also have many different views on what constitutes being a parent.) At times staff have needed to back off and accept the fact that professionals or paid workers, as we call them, do not have to be the only providers of services, nor are they necessarily the best at group-facilitating, engaging new parents or home-visiting.

The parent-run playgroup at Pen Green has a more active group of parent volunteers than the nursery. This is perhaps because the transition from parent to voluntary worker is easier to envisage than the transition from parent to paid worker. It might also be that the style of working adopted by playgroup leaders makes them more approachable (Watt, 1977).

Getting parents involved from the beginning

From the beginning parents made decisions about how rooms should be used, which services got priority, how services were delivered and by whom. Parents interviewed for all staff appointments. As a local authority service there were clearly tensions between what we as a staff group wanted to put up for negotiation with parents and what the funding agencies considered appropriate. The centre could not be turned into a home for the elderly, parents (women) could not refuse admission to other parents (men) on a gender basis, nor could they exclude elements within the community which many parents thought were undesirable, such as drug users.

Some parents wanted a greater focus on work with older children (often those parents whose children had left nursery); others wanted more provision for the under-twos (usually those parents with toddlers and babies). Discussions on all these issues took place in a variety of forums. There were parents' meetings in the evening once a month, family group meetings during the day once every six weeks, home visits or individual sessions with staff. There was also the policy group meeting where parents and staff met with senior managers and – as a last resort – occasional public confrontations in the corridor between an irate parent and a member of staff.

Developing quality partnerships between parents and staff

The quality of the relationship which developed between staff and parents really seemed to depend on the openness, clarity, and warmth displayed by each individual member of staff. On some of our first home visits to families in the community we were told that:

> . . . social workers are the welfare, they take your kids away . . . health visitors tell you what's supposed to be good for your child . . . and teachers tell you in five minutes what it's taken you five years to find out about your child!

These were the stereotypes we were working against! Watt points out that 'the control' element is always there in parent/staff relationships, since some staff decisions are non-negotiable. It has pleasantly surprised us over the years to discover how many issues can be usefully put up for discussion.

Individual parents have sometimes challenged our rights as a staff group to make decisions and have sometimes resented our refusal to compromise. This is an inevitable consequence of attempting a partnership. We have taken these challenges on board positively and have constantly needed to go back and re-appraise our decisions and see if they are still relevant or appropriate over time. It is important to ask ourselves: 'Do we still need to do it like that?', or 'Why did we *ever* do it like that?' . . .

Staff at Pen Green also had to get used to working with tensions between workers and parents, parents and children, workers and line managers. We needed to have a solid structure to our work but we also needed to be flexible so that we could respond to parents, to the changing needs of the local community and to the changing needs of children using the centre. Boundaries could sometimes be waived. For example, at the centre, parents were limited to phoning from the public office but if a parent needed to make a very personal call they could use a private room; or a child's clearly defined nursery sessions would be changed if a parent was having a difficult pregnancy.

Responsiveness was not without its problems; sometimes parents would ask staff for quick decisions while walking down a corridor; sometimes parents would choose to ask a member of staff who they thought would give them the answer they wanted and avoid staff with clearer boundaries; sometimes staff gave contradictory messages. What we were aiming at was *clarity*, some degree of *fairness*, *accountability* (so that decisions were always explained verbally or in writing), and having the grace to say we were sorry when we got it wrong.

The parents' view of the nursery and the impact of staff knowing these views

Pen Green staff and students collected comments from parents on their relationship with staff:

> When (Diane) was in nursery it was really good, a place where I could go and meet people, you got to know the staff.

This mother's views changed, however, when her child moved on to school and she continued to attend groups at the centre:

Some staff I like, some I don't. I think they're quite snobby.

The relationship that parents had with their child's family worker was very special. One mother felt that the beginning and end of nursery sessions just didn't give parents the time they needed to give feedback to staff.

I used to come to the Parents' Council Meeting which is held once a month and any parent can come whose children are in the nursery. I found it was a good place to air my grievances, or even suggest things that could be beneficial to them and to us . . . other parents used to come to me, too frightened to do it themselves. Eventually I became a chairwoman of this meeting. I have been able to put a few points that have not made major changes but just little points that helped other parents and myself to get what they want out of Pen Green. When one of my daughters was in the nursery she had a family worker and I found that I didn't always have any time to talk with the family worker about anything; she was always very busy. When my other daughter started in the nursery I eventually put forward at one of the Parents' Council Meetings that I thought it would be a good idea if perhaps once a month we could have a special time set when we could meet with the family worker on her own, out of the nursery environment, in a room where the parents and the worker could sit quietly and talk without any interruptions from children or other parents, and it has been in operation for the last three years now.
(Santos, 1992)

What this parent saw as only a minor change actually impacted enormously on nursery staff. We realised for the first time that although *we* knew which parents and children were linked with which member of staff in the nursery, the parents didn't actually know each other. The family group meetings that we then set up gave each parent the chance to meet the parents of many of their children's friends, and an opportunity to discuss nursery and centre issues more intimately, in an environment in which they felt much less vulnerable. Not all parents found dialogue with staff very easy. One said that she 'took criticisms away and let them fester'; another stated that, 'you've got to really make your statement and stick by it and not get sucked into other people's stuff'. This illustrated the kind of group pressure that parents could experience when something problematic was going on. Another parent said:

I felt people had time for me and I felt the staff were very approachable if you had a problem. It's a two way thing. I feel it is more of a family unit here.

You get told quite a lot . . . And I get asked my opinion, 'Do you think it is a good idea to do such and such?' It is nice to be consulted about things. I know quite everything that is going on here, and if you ask, you get what you want to know.

Of course, we didn't always get it right:

As a parent in these (early) days I feel perhaps we could have been consulted a lot more than we were. In those days things could happen without you knowing that they were going to happen.

Most parents were very generous with their feedback;

I don't expect them (the staff) to agree all the time, but I expect them at least to listen to and give me a fair chance, or perhaps even discuss it further. If I do make a comment then I do expect an answer. I don't go away feeling that I haven't achieved anything, even if it is just being listened to. When I was not too confident I used to go away feeling that it was a waste of time, but I got fed up feeling like that, so I became a bit more assertive . . .

What we wanted

We aimed for a partnership with parents which was equal, active and responsible (Nicholl, 1986). This meant that we needed to be 'confident and secure professionals' (Tomlinson, 1986), well-trained in our own profession and able to co-operate and work in an integrated way with other agencies.

However, as Ian Sparks (1985) points out, the process by which frontline workers engage parents and children may not be replicated in the way that they themselves are line-managed. There were many difficulties for us as a staff group trying to be enabling, consciously avoiding 'over professionalising' the services we offered (which wasn't the same thing as disowning our professional knowledge and experience), working participatively and co-operatively within our own organisation and yet being line-managed by a fairly traditional, male-dominated, local government bureaucracy.

We had the additional problem that our issues were often not the principal concern of one department, but straddled two or three departments who weren't used to talking to each other and often didn't appear to speak the same language. While we have received considerable support from some officers in Education, Social Services and Health Departments, our own feeling, shared by colleagues in similar situations (Gilkes, 1987) is that a lot of positive multi-disciplinary work gets buried at about middle management level. Penn and Riley (1992) point out the need for a change within attitudes in local government departments in a chapter entitled 'Co-operation, co-ordination and confusion'.

IDEOLOGY IN PRACTICE:
WHAT WE SET UP AT PEN GREEN

The services which we set up at Pen Green were organic and not fixed in time. Our ideology has been constant. Many of the groups, activities and programmes that were set up for, or by, parents and children have been written about in some detail by researchers who spent time with us (Pugh, 1987, 1988; Widlake, 1986; Santos, 1992) and by staff who are increasingly undertaking their own practitioner research and are getting it published.

No rigorous conceptual framework was ever laid down by the LEA or the centre's steering/policy group. No one had addressed the tensions involved in placing a service which was technically 'open' (like nursery education) alongside a service which focused on child protection (such as day care and family work). Departmental priorities were still sufficiently blurred in the early eighties, for the centre to go its own way. We were left relatively free to respond to the demands made on us.

Our work had four main strands as can be seen in figure 4 on page 20. These included:

- the community nursery;
- family work;
- health work;
- adult and community education.

Many of the activities we have undertaken stem from, or feed into, each other and many involved joint work with other agencies or with the voluntary sector. Although not all of these activities were set up in 1983 each strand was addressed simultaneously since we were aiming to give parents and children as many different ways into the centre as possible. We wanted to make it easy for parents and children to move through the centre so that those who perceived themselves as 'clients' (who had been referred by another agency)

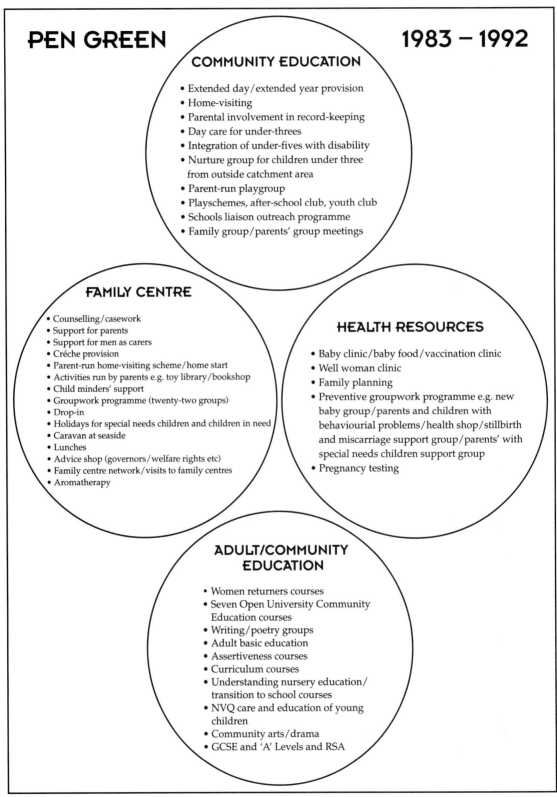

PEN GREEN   **1983 – 1992**

COMMUNITY EDUCATION

- Extended day/extended year provision
- Home-visiting
- Parental involvement in record-keeping
- Day care for under-threes
- Integration of under-fives with disability
- Nurture group for children under three from outside catchment area
- Parent-run playgroup
- Playschemes, after-school club, youth club
- Schools liaison outreach programme
- Family group/parents' group meetings

FAMILY CENTRE

- Counselling/casework
- Support for parents
- Support for men as carers
- Créche provision
- Parent-run home-visiting scheme/home start
- Activities run by parents e.g. toy library/bookshop
- Child minders' support
- Groupwork programme (twenty-two groups)
- Drop-in
- Holidays for special needs children and children in need
- Caravan at seaside
- Lunches
- Advice shop (governors/welfare rights etc)
- Family centre network/visits to family centres
- Aromatherapy

HEALTH RESOURCES

- Baby clinic/baby food/vaccination clinic
- Well woman clinic
- Family planning
- Preventive groupwork programme e.g. new baby group/parents and children with behaviourial problems/health shop/stillbirth and miscarriage support group/parents' with special needs children support group
- Pregnancy testing

ADULT/COMMUNITY EDUCATION

- Women returners courses
- Seven Open University Community Education courses
- Writing/poetry groups
- Adult basic education
- Assertiveness courses
- Curriculum courses
- Understanding nursery education/transition to school courses
- NVQ care and education of young children
- Community arts/drama
- GCSE and 'A' Levels and RSA

Figure 4   The four main strands of work undertaken at Pen Green between 1983–1992

and parents who had just walked in the door, could each make their own choices in their own time about how and in what way they got involved.

In this way a teenager with a new baby might start to use the baby clinic which was run very informally with big cushions, sagbags, easy chairs and toys for the children. Volunteers were on hand to make coffee, health visitors were available to offer counselling and support; and digital scales were provided so that parents could weigh their own babies. She might then meet some other young parents and decide to join an Open University study group during the day; or she might work with the pack on 'Living with Babies and Toddlers' in the evening. She might feel later that her toddler wanted company and different kinds of play provision and might join a parent and toddler session either run by nursery staff and community service volunteers or by nursery staff and parents. There, in comfortable, roomy surroundings, very young children get the chance to explore with clay, sand and paint more freely than would be possible at home. In this way parents decide how they use the centre.

Carrie was seventeen years old when she first came to Pen Green and in the extract below she describes the choices she made about her level of involvement with the centre:

> Lizzie, my daughter, was four weeks old when I was introduced to the Pen Green Centre in 1987.
>
> Baby Weigh-In – *Many mums find this an easy way into the centre. It is also a good way for people to become a person, not just a mum.*
>
> Mother & Baby – *this group has been one of my favourite groups as I learnt how to play with and how to enjoy my daughter.*
>
> Single Parents – *A very good support in my life. I have made lots of new friends and found that I am not the only one finding the ups and downs of single parenthood straining.*
>
> Stillbirth & Neo-Natal Death – *This group has been a very sad, happy and loving group to me. I was able to touch and release pains that had made me feel depressed. Many women come to just talk about their babies and cry or laugh about their lives.*
>
> Writers' Group – *At the moment about seven people use this group. We either share our written work or we try to enlarge our knowledge on writers.*

Parents who had come into the centre requesting a nursery place might also decide that they wanted something for themselves and use the family room or drop-in. They might start to use the drop-in on a regular basis and make new friends. For some parents the drop-in was a sanctuary where they could take a break, have a foot massage or get some support: for others it was a place where they got information or got involved in a specific piece of group work lasting several weeks. There was always a family worker in the room so that parents had access to a listening ear if they needed it. The family room worker also ensured that the drop-in was a safe and interesting place for both parents and children.

How well does it work?

Conflicting needs of parents and children

Sometimes parents' and children's needs conflicted. Since some parents needed to smoke, the atmosphere in the family room was often very unhealthy. As a staff group we had to balance the needs of isolated, often vulnerable parents who smoked continuously at home and who used the family room for many hours a week, against our increasing awareness of the dangers of passive smoking for young children. A visiting Director of Education in 1984, who'd only been in the centre a matter of minutes, told us that the first thing he'd do would be to ban smoking in the centre. We felt that this would be a bit like scoring a home goal. It would certainly reduce our workload since many of the parents who needed the centre told us that they would stop using it if smoking was banned. Smoking in the family room continues to be a difficult issue for us, one that is not easily reconcilable with good child-care practice. The latest compromise that we have negotiated with parents is that there is a non-smoking period between half past eleven and one o'clock when parents and children are sharing a meal in the family room. (Smoking has never been allowed in the nursery, creche, baby rooms or nursery dining areas.)

Parent participation

The family room or drop-in, has at times been seen as the barometer of parent involvement in the centre. Initially, some of the parents who used it most seemed to be fairly oblivious to the needs of other parents. However, as they got more involved in the centre, for example by showing visitors round, chairing a parents' meeting, or by representing other parents in a family group meeting or at a conference, they seemed better able to take on the struggle of others (Santos, 1992).

Learning how to let go and share childcare

Parents who began to use the family room or drop-in when they settled their children into nursery were given a chance to get in touch with how they felt about 'letting go' of their child and trusting him or her into the nursery staff's care. We invited new parents to attend a series of sessions on 'letting go' and sharing the care of their children and we had a very experienced outside consultant who had previously worked for Child and Family Guidance, running the session alongside nursery workers. Many parents (twenty-seven out of thirty-three new parents in 1991) used these sessions as part of *their* own transition experience. For some women the short break offered by a few nursery sessions was the first bit of time they had had on their own for several years. A child starting nursery was experienced as either a cause for celebration or as a bereavement. Both positions were respected by staff.

Using facilities to the full

Parents were made aware of what was on offer through a variety of booklets and leaflets which were given out on home visits, initial visits to the centre and by colleagues in other agencies. Many colleagues in Social Services, or the Area Health Authority, while offering some of their time to us to co-run groups or clinics, also referred families that they worked with to the centre. In this way a health visitor who co-ran a baby group at the centre for parents and babies might encourage families in her case load to attend as well. A psychiatrist giving his time to undertake staff supervision might also refer several of his patients to a survivors' group. A social worker from the disability services co-running a group to support parents with children with special needs, might also have referred children on her case load to a holiday play-scheme. This meant that we could work closely with professional colleagues and offer them a reciprocal deal for their time and experience.

Making it work: a balancing act for parents, staff and colleagues from other agencies

As a staff group we continually have to balance the needs of children and parents (both local families and increasingly, families with children in need from the rest of the town). Our colleagues in other agencies whose expertise is vitally important to us also have to justify the time they spend with us against their increasing case loads. Parents too, have to carve out time for themselves, and find time to be with their children against increasing pressures to take on part-time work or work double shifts to supplement incomes which become smaller and smaller.

We all share a belief in inter-agency collaboration; that the services we provide should be open to *all* families and that power needs to be shared in:

> *a society which encourages all to believe in themselves. That means valuing them for themselves and genuinely opening opportunities for melioration. In such a buoyant milieu, teachers would be able to find the button marked self-esteem in more of their pupils, aspirations would be higher, employers would expect more of their workers and offer much more, and I have little doubt that the Health and Social Services would be dealing far less with the effects of depression and despair . . .*
> (Tomlinson, 1991)

3 THE COMMUNITY NURSERY 1983–5

LETTING CHILDREN GROW

When children have no autonomy in learning everyone is likely to be bored
(Hawkins, 1965)

Let me grow up as I am!
Try to understand why I need to be as I am
Not how my mother wants me to be,
Nor how my father hopes I will be,
Nor how my teacher thinks I ought to be,
Please try to understand me and help me to grow up,
Like this, just as I am!
(Anonymous Brazilian poem used by early-years' educators)

Rigid structures imposed on children without reference to the context in which the child is living and learning are dangerous. We wanted to make the children's concerns our concerns. We wanted to encourage children to believe they could make things happen, supported by, but not dependent on, us. Janet Moyles (1989) comments on how important it is for children to experience getting things wrong. We need a whole new vocabulary in early-years' education for experiences that 'don't work out': a whole new vocabulary to describe children's approach to their own learning. This could then result in a whole new way for parents to greet children when they collect them from nursery or school.

Imagine, as our colleague Patrick Whittacker (an education consultant) did, this scenario: a child is greeted by her parents with the enquiry, 'Lovely to have you home . . . how many mistakes did you make today?' as opposed to 'Were you good?' or 'Did you do what you were told?' The child's school report might read:

It's a delight to have Sophie in the class, she is such an adventurous *child; so* forthright *in her manner; so* persistent *in the face of opposition. She* challenged *my thinking in many areas and comes to school full of problems that* she *wants to sort out. Sophie has an* active *mind and I'm pleased to say that* she talks a great deal *about things that interest her and shares her ideas with the rest of the class. It is* inspiring *to see her* anger *with anything she perceives as an injustice, such as cruelty to animals or bullying in the playground.*

It would be inaccurate to say that when the centre was set up in 1983 everything was up for examination. In reality we held from the start certain principles about how children learn. Our primary concern was with the development of self-esteem in children. It was enshrined in our curriculum document, which was completed after we had been open several years. It states:

> *Children should feel strong*
> *Children should feel in control*
> *Children should feel able to question*
> *Children should feel able to choose.*

STAFF

Appointing staff

It is important to look back to those first nursery staff who were appointed between January and April 1983 because who they were and what they had to offer provided a scaffolding which moved the nursery on from the paper brief of the policy makers. The whole centre had only seven staff in the first instance, since no-one knew how much the adult education, family work, and parental involvement aspects of the provision would develop.

   The first staff group had a mixed bag of qualifications and experience. Most of them stayed for five to six years, not because they didn't have choices but because they were able to develop their careers within the establishment (through training, promotion or the creation of new posts to run new services). The head of centre, with a background in teaching and experience in community social work, was complemented by a principal social worker post, filled by a social worker with a post-graduate teachers' certificate in nursery education. The senior teacher/family worker in the nursery had a post-graduate teachers' certificate and had worked in workplace and community nurseries in London, rather than completing her probationary year in main stream schools. As each member of staff was appointed the appointments' panel increased in size. Everyone wanted representation on the panel and community representatives and subsequently parent representatives, were always included.

Valuing life experience *and* qualifications

We established a policy of valuing life experiences as well as qualifications and decided to avoid appointing nursery nurses straight from college. All the nursery nurses we did appoint had previous experience in residential schools, special schools, with child and family guidance, or had worked as nannies (often overseas). We also appointed staff with other kinds of higher education or training such as women with hard-won Open University degrees.

The life experiences which staff have brought to the centre such as working in playgroups, managing private day nurseries, working in industry and being foster parents have provided a rich backdrop which has enhanced their professional qualifications.

It has always seemed important to try and attract staff *back* who have older chidren of their own and to support young staff who want to job share after taking maternity leave. In our efforts to employ men in the nursery we have had to re-consider once again the issue of appropriate qualifications and experience. We have tried to appoint men with aptitude and alternative kinds of life experience and training as happens in child-care services in Denmark.

The need for reflective, informed practitioners

The demands we make on staff in the nursery to read widely, to reflect on their own practice, to keep detailed records and to undertake practitioner research make it increasingly unlikely that applicants without further or higher education qualifications in early-years education and care could be appointed. We keep our options open, however, and advertise accordingly in as wide a range of health, education and social work journals as we can manage so that we can attract staff who want a different kind of challenge.

We registered with CEYA (the Council for Early Years Awards) in 1993 so that we could encourage unqualified volunteers (such as playgroup workers and parent helpers) to undertake National Vocational Qualifications (NVQ) in childcare and education which we would see as one possible *starting point* for a career in education or day care. We also linked with Northamptonshire's licensed teacher programme on one occasion, as it made it possible for us to complement the many years of work and study an existing member of the nursery staff had undertaken, resulting in the achievement of qualified teacher status. This member of staff has now embarked on an MEd and sees qualified teacher status as a starting point for further studies in early-years education.

With the wide variety of modular BTech courses available at the local colleges, new doors are opening for women and men wanting to work in early-years settings. Our policy is to keep abreast of all these new developments and we are wary of any that look like short cuts to, or substitutes for, the highest possible standards of training for early-years educators.

Working with young children requires real intellectual rigour. The kind of training and experience that we consider to be appropriate, could never be achieved in one year's training. Early-years educators need to be able to make continuous observations of children whilst establishing and maintaining an appropriately stimulating and demanding educational provision for them. They need to have a sound understanding of how children learn and how children's learning can best be supported and extended. They need to be clear about equal opportunities issues and child protection issues, to have a knowledge of current early-years research and an awareness of new developments in their specialist field (Curtis and Hevey, 1992). They need to love children, and enjoy working with them.

What we asked for

Whatever their background all our early appointed staff had two things in common. They had all answered advertisements which specified that the job would involve working with children *and* parents, and they were all women. Our first adverts seem very laboured now.

> *Teacher/family worker required to work as a member of a professional team within the Pen Green Centre in Corby. The centre is an exciting new venture providing an integrated multi-disciplinary service to meet the needs of approximately seventy children and their families.*

Unlike colleagues in centres we visited in London, we were not allowed to use the title 'family worker' exclusively, but had to link it to the traditional professional qualification of whichever post we had available. In fact, all posts at the centre were initially advertised as family worker posts, whether the vacancy was for a teaching post, a social worker or a nursery nurse. The job specification emphasised innovative work, non-traditional hours and home-visiting and raised the issue of training and supervision for all staff. (Supervision was an unfamiliar word to educationalists in the eighties.) Nursery staff were advised that their role was that of enabling children and encouraging and supporting parents.

Staff beliefs: philosophical influences (chart on pages 30–32)

Some staff (principally the teachers) had been influenced by training and mainstream school experience which emphasised a Plowden-style sixties, child-centred approach. Papers and reports which we wrote in those early days reflected this influence.

> *What a good and wise Father desires for all his children, a nation must desire for all its children.*
> (Haddow, 1933)

However, when we used this as a public statement of staff views we changed it to read:

> *What a good and wise* parent *desires for* his or her *own children, a nation must desire for all its children!*

At Pen Green we were working to secure the kind of community nursery which educational visionaries like Christian Schiller had envisaged. Schiller was an HMI (Her Majesty's Inspector) and senior lecturer in Primary Education at the Institute of Education at the University of London and he stated:

> *When I peer into the future I don't see any army of professionals at all. I doubt very much if we shall need primary schools as we think of them today. What I see in every small community (a few streets, maybe one street) is a building; the community's building, and it will be a place to which young children come to play, to explore, to learn. There will be facilities there, resources there, far greater than can be provided in any one home. And there will be teachers there to help, teachers who are there as leaders. And Mum will come there and feel at home, and Dad and the neighbour next door, and they'll understand and they will help, from time to time.*
> (Schiller, 1979, pp. 104–5)

Several of our staff in the early days had come to work with very young children, having trained to work with an older age range. They were attracted to working with children in an innovative early-years provision. One teacher had come to Northamptonshire from a nursery in the Greater London Council

	1983–85	1985–87	1987–90	1990 onwards
Philosophical influences	Plowden, 'Child-Centred', Christian Schiller, Paulo Freire, informal adult education, community social work. GLC community nurseries	Community education. Cumberledge – health. Multi-disciplinary approach. Gender work; equal opportunities policies; Strathclydes joint approach	Athey, Bruce, Margaret McMillan	Children Act, Education Reform Act. Italian Pedagogy. Visits to Denmark. Bruce. *Starting With Quality*, report, (DES, 1990)
Practical influences	Labour controlled county council. Forty-three per cent male unemployment. No facilities for women and children. Run down estate. Two-thirds single parent mothers	Conservative county council. Large numbers of referrals for one–two and a half year-olds. Huge waiting-list. Women working twilight and weekends	New housing, shops 'done up'. Male unemployment drops, part-time work for women increases. Increased vandalism. Erosion of community health services	Fire/vandalism. Poll tax. Poverty. Increased use of centre by men. 1993, Labour control county council again
Management style	Power-sharing. Co-operative, 'everything' open for negotiation. Challenge is experienced positively	More awareness of need for firm boundaries/clarity. Constant need to explore issues of working as a team. Use of outside consultant for trouble-shooting	All senior staff finally go on management training! More work on boundaries. Clearer about need for staff support and staff supervision and the difference between the two. A 'sidearchy'	More awareness of gender issues within senior staff. Need to take time out to plan. Some conflict avoidance still
Staff attitude	All women staff, wide experience of statutory and voluntary sector. Policy of appointing staff with relevant experience and education or care qualifications	Male and female staff group. Gender training. Race awareness training. Parents and clients can be service providers. Women staff encouraged to job-share after maternity leave	**NOT** doing 'to' or 'for' parents. Playschemes offered for staff's children	Complementary expertise. Staff believe parents are committed to their children's education
Beliefs about children	Need for family groups across ages. Community-based nursery with home visits for all families. Children make decisions, challenging, choosing	All children benefit from some nursery education/care; autonomy valued. Being strong/children needing to be assertive. Child protection programme. Children as decision makers	Focus on equal opportunities. Child's view-point vital. Children have a right to have their needs met. Whether starting point is emotional or cognitive	Children's right to education and care in their own community. No assumptions about class and disadvantage. Importance of the group as well as the individual

Figure 5   Philosophical and practical influences affect management style, staff attitudes, beliefs, values and pedagogy

	1983–85	1985–87	1987–90	1990 onwards
Pedagogy – how we are teaching the children, how children learn, how their learning develops and how we extend their play	Emphasis on first hand experience, celebrations. Content looked traditional but how the children used it wasn't	HMI videos of Northern Ireland focus on nursery as a workshop. Emphasis on basic materials, clay, sand and water. Child's right to join in or *not* honoured and to have her work protected. Uninterrupted play sessions, emphasis on process	Nursery becomes a workshop. Discover 'schemas'. Staff search for a language. Training with Athey and Bruce. Increased need to communicate our practice to parents	Interactionist – see the children in context. Children need to feel in control. Staff discuss physics
Beliefs about parents	Need for assertiveness training. 'Good enough parenting', is OK. Some parent education, supporting parents in their parenting. Parents' evening meetings	Realisation that values about bringing up children largely culturally determined. Parents are the primary carers. Parents are not a homogenous group	Need to inform parents. Plethora of legislation affecting family life. Need information *from* parents. Parents want to study	Need for a responsive and accessible complaints procedure. Access issues for minority groups, access issues for men
Parents' role in the centre	Help in nursery and value home visits. Drop-in groups set up, parents interviewing staff. Fund-raising. On committees	Parents run crèches, toy libraries, playgroups. Parents as paid workers	Parents in the nursery groups. First GCSEs. Parents very active in community action group. Protests, join in on march to county hall	Parents run groups, attend seminars, share experiences with teachers. First 'A' Levels. Women *and* men studying
Focus	Home-visiting. Community visits and links with other agencies. Joint inter-agency training courses set up	Urban Aid funding. Expansion, Outreach Projects. After-school club, youth club, family holidays	Consolidation and communication. Ensuring quality	Record-keeping. Research. Staff's needs are important. Survival and enrichment
Social/ recreational holidays	Mini-bus for holidays/recreation. Youth hostelling. Family holidays at seaside	Own mini-bus full-time. After-school club five–eleven year olds holidays. Butlins for Centre family holidays	Special-needs parents' group, family holidays. Buy a caravan at seaside for any family to use cheaply	Single parents to Château in France. Caravan holiday. Special needs parents' group holiday

Figure 5   (continued)

	1983–85	1985–87	1987–90	1990 onwards
Community links	Community arts. Action group against Centre. Exchanges with schools. Playgroup established at Centre. Community mornings and lunches for volunteers and professional colleagues	Parent's rooms in three schools. After-school club set up and youth club. Combined Centres' association. Family Centre network, home-visiting service set-up. Celebrations/carnivals/ art events	Two outreach groups set up. RNIB school exchanges and visits	Strong links with PPA Welfare Rights, Volunteer Bureau. Voluntary organisations concerned with children with disability
Involvement with other agencies	Strong links with health visitors, child and family guidance. High level involvement, local patch team, social services	Health visitor seconded to staff group. Other health visitors help. Baby clinics. Well woman clinics etc set up. County multi-disciplinary training course. Close link with adult psychiatric services	High level health visitor involvement. Good GP links. Strong links with adult psychiatric services. Child and family guidance	Improved link with social services long-term and intake teams. Greater inter-agency partnership to cater for 'children in need' throughout the town
Record-keeping and assessment	Staff take developmental assessment check-lists and share them with parents at home. Regular home-visiting	Child studies made in detail. Observation sheets introduced. Parents encouraged to look at children's file	Dynamic observations rather than check-lists. Parents begin record-keeping	'Celebration of achievement' files set up. PLOD charts in use (possible lines of development)
Quality assurance	Parents nominally on policy group. User-group set up and well used in evening	Parents more active on policy group. Users' group very vocal. Minutes circulated to all parents	Parents council. Family group meetings set up. (Crèche provided for evening meetings and daytime meetings)	Internal complaints procedures in place. Consultation exercises. Monthly parents group and family group. Parents regularly visit other Centres and evaluate

Figure 5   (continued)

where staff had successfully broken down some of the barriers between home and school.

Other staff had been strongly influenced by Kohl, Holt and Illich, and by Sylvia Ashton-Warner and Paulo Freire who argue for the importance of the context in which children and adults are living and the emotional side of learning. Both reject imposed educational systems which fragment the learning experience and make it dull and irrelevant.

> *It's not beauty to abruptly halt the growth of a young mind and to overlay it with the frame of an imposed culture.*
> (Ashton-Warner, 1963, p. 34)

One of the strongest philosophical influences on subsequent developments was that staff with a social work background had adopted 'a community social work approach' such as that advocated by Holman (1983). They didn't see parents who experienced difficulties with their children as 'problem parents' but rather as parents with problems. Many of these problems were directly linked with poverty and unemployment. They felt that the nursery should be accessible, offering community nursery provision to local children, with services which reflected the needs of the children's families and the wider community. The importance of maintaining the nursery (and in those early days the rest of the centre) as a local resource for local families was seen as essential by staff who fully understood how a nursery could become a kind of catalystic focus for community action (Ryan, 1986).

Then and now it seemed essential to staff that we should approach *all* families who wanted to use the nursery in the same way. All families who wanted nursery places were to be home-visited before a decision was made about who should be offered what. This was irrespective of whether the family had been referred to us by a health visitor and a social worker or whether they had simply walked in the door enquiring about the nursery.

All parents were given the same application form, which asked them what they wanted in terms of hours, how much time they would like to spend with their child in the nursery and what activities they might like for themselves. We realised fairly quickly, when parents failed to fill in this section, that because they were unaccustomed to going into schools (one of the local schools still had a line parents weren't supposed to cross), we would need to outline the type of activities that could be made available, such as parents' discussion groups, a drop-in, and baby clinics.

THE BUILDING AT PEN GREEN

The building which was to house the centre was old and abandoned and at first seemed totally unsuitable as a place in which to set up a nursery for young children. There was a very large school hall with no windows at child-height; a long corridor with a number of smaller rooms coming off each side; and one reasonably large room which had formerly housed a dental clinic.

The ceiling in the main hall was incredibly high. As our finances were limited, it was only possible to give the impression that the height of the ceiling had been reduced in one corner of the room. This was achieved with the equivalent of horizontally hung Venetian blinds. The high ceiling did not seem to daunt the children. For them it was much more important that the room was broken up into bays which could be made more home-like, so we introduced a large number of dividers, at just about child-height. Large open areas were left, however, enabling climbing equipment to be available at all times. Many parents were worried about letting their children play outside alone due to traffic and other worries. While a few of the nursery children were playing out and walking up to the shops early in the morning and fairly late at night, other nursery children never got to play outside at all unless they were at the nursery. We felt that we had to bring the outside in, so that even when it was cold or wet children could play, climb and slide energetically.

We worked hard to make the building children-friendly by pushing the LEA to find additional funding for low windows. At least these meant that children could see the outside world, perhaps watch their friends spray-painting the snow outside or just have an awareness of the light changing on a winter afternoon.

We also created a fairly intimate home-corner out of a large cupboard, turning the builders' incompetence to our advantage. An exposed pipe was neatly turned into a set of carpeted steps at the entrance to this 'retreat' which delighted climbing toddlers. Perhaps because it all seemed so awful when we arrived, but so spacious, we were able to think freely and not allow the architecture to dictate how we organised the environment.

By the time we had visited many purpose-built nurseries which had restricted space for children's play and the equivalent of boxrooms for staff and parents, we felt more positive about our own vast area.

Because no final decisions had been made about how the rooms should be used before the first parents and children arrived, they felt powerful and were able to make themselves heard. They were consulted and their views led us to revise many of our own. Carpets had not been laid, the concrete was still drying, alterations were still being made and the public, mainly women and children, were being invited in. Visits to other centres while the builders were still working, meant that we could come back, and review decisions and change paper plans which had been made without reference to either staff or the community.

It became a standing joke that the architect would see the head of centre coming towards him at County Hall and dart into any available lift. The building presented us with a diverse range of problems which were the result of its age, and former usage. The building specifications had been drawn up by officers in the Education Department with little awareness of the needs of parents or children under three. At one point we had to stand bodily in the way of the plasterers and joiners who were about to cut in half the only sizeable space left for parents. The wall they were about to erect would have left one end of the available space as a small square room for staff, and the other end a small square room for parents! For several years we had sinks at both ends of what became the family room to remind us of this altercation. We were not to have our own staff room until 1992 when some staff, returning from a visit to Denmark, insisted that we really could not do without one.

Our ever-changing use of space

The principle that nothing about the building was fixed and that most things were up for negotiation has remained. Even in the first three years, rooms changed their usage in response to the changing needs of children, parents or staff. One small side room which was set aside for children to use as a quiet room was changed – by the nursery children – into a second home-corner. It was then purloined by parents and re-named the 'wet room', and with its soft, subdued wallpaper, sofas and chairs, became a place where adults could rest or have a cry. It then became a multi-purpose office, technically for the head and deputy but also for supervision and support sessions, case conferences, breast-feeding and so on. In 1992, it was transformed into a 'snoezelen' – a sniffing and dozing room: a soft, soothing environment for the nursery children, for aromatherapy, massage and relaxation. These facilities are also occasionally borrowed by 'stressed-out' parents and staff! It is used on a daily basis by an increasing number of special-needs support groups, special schools, the adult-training centre and individual parents of children with special needs.

Other rooms have also had memorable life histories. A urinal became a very small staff room; then a clothes store; then a health food shop (a disastrous endeavour); then a second-hand clothes store; and then a toy library. It is now a nicely decorated 'advice shop' run by parent volunteers and is a refuge for well-established parents wanting somewhere to study, chat or smoke when the family room is over-occupied.

The building in relation to the children

The size of the space we had for the children's nursery was daunting and a challenge. What concerned us most was how it would affect the youngest children, since our provision was supposed to cater for children from nought to five years. We visited several combined nursery centres with baby rooms on the day nursery model and felt uncomfortable with the idea of separating children simply because they were under three. It reinforced the division between education (for the over-threes) and care (for the under-threes).

We focused on making comfortable, cosy withdrawal areas in the nursery and rooms down the corridor for quiet times or rests. We created areas where the more vulnerable children could be protected from hugely energetic and expressive three and four-year-olds.

One group of staff returned from a visit to a centre with a 'baby den' and a nursery where they had observed a group of younger toddlers peeping over the top of the door which separated them. These children desperately wanted to join the nursery children in the next room who were involved in 'educational activities'. This confirmed our decision to focus more on setting up 'family groups' as a source of security and comfort for all the children. Instead of separating children by age we decided that small numbers of children (ten families in all with about six children in each session) would be attached to one family worker who would be their 'special person' for the whole time the child was in nursery. Younger siblings would benefit from being in the same family group as their sisters or brothers.

> If we want workers who are not afraid of bodily warmth, cuddling and of making intimate relationships with the children in their care, we need to introduce key worker systems that will allow these relationships to form.
> (Calder, 1990 (b), p. 23)

Our decision to use family groups rather than having a baby room, toddler room and pre-school room was also a result of the constraints of relative room sizes. Our resistance to containing young children in the small rooms we observed in many day nurseries and some combined centres has been affirmed recently by observing provision for nought to three-year-olds in northern Italy. There, the very youngest nursery children are encouraged to roam in safe open spaces which they do with enormous enjoyment. They are also, in this very safe environment, allowed to move away from 'the ever watchful eye of the adult'. Although our own open spaces were not the result of the planned 'pedagogical architecture' (Rouse, 1991) so strikingly apparent in Italian nurseries, they were very important for the children. With a building which was so obviously not purpose built, staff found it very difficult to relax when children did move out of sight, down corridors or into a side room. Our interventions were respectful. Children were allowed, encouraged even, to be independent and autonomous without adults hindering them but most of us felt we lost pounds in the first few months, chasing round the building to keep children in sight! Over time, our vigilance has not decreased but we have become more trusting and the building has been made considerably safer.

Principles influence practice and use of space

It is already possible to see how our basic principles about children affected decisions about the architecture and the proposed allocation of rooms within the building. We tried to give children space in which to run and be free. At the same time small rooms, dens and private home-corners were created so that children could feel intimate and get away from adults. We were also very aware of the need for children to feel in control of their separation and individuation (Mahler, Pine and Bergman, 1980). This meant that there also had to be areas in the nursery where adults could feel relaxed and valued; where they could sit on comfortable adult-sized chairs; where there was a table for magazines and newspapers and where parents could sit with an adult friend and yet be very close to their child.

PARENTS LETTING GO & CHILDREN SETTLING IN

We decided to establish a two-week settling-in period for all children, as one of our relatively inflexible boundaries. Two weeks seemed a safe period within which most children would find the confidence to gradually move away from their care-giver and start to make a relationship of trust with their family worker. The care-giver, sometimes a parent, a grandparent or childminder (but always an adult), would be available if needed. Some children found the transition relatively unproblematic and their parents could move out of the nursery within a few days and drop in to the family room for a coffee or a smoke – close by but not actually in sight. Some children needed to stay very close to their parent for the full two weeks. Sometimes parents weren't ready to let children go and on some occasions two weeks just wasn't enough. It was important for us that the parent gave a commitment to stay as part of their contract with the nursery.

> *This is just as he wants it*
> *A little at a time, of each new thing, is best*
> *Too much and too sudden is too frightening.*
> (Ted Hughes, 1976)

This policy had been challenged as much by professional colleagues as by parents. True, some parents have complained that it has caused them practical difficulties but somehow they have always been able to arrange to take holiday time, if in work. Some have shared the load with a partner or grandparent.

When parents have younger siblings it has been important that we accept their presence in the nursery and that we make appropriate provision for them as well as nursery children. Some parents have chosen to make this a special time and have left siblings with friends or relatives so that they can give individual attention to the child who is entering nursery. We are also very flexible about start dates which can be at any time of the year but are chiefly between August and October.

Separation anxiety affects both the child and the parent and to some extent the family worker. During this period all three feel inadequate and vulnerable at times and we have had to find ways of supporting everyone concerned. Sometimes parents would bribe with sweets or leave children angrily and inappropriately. Sometimes family workers would mishandle an intervention and move in too quickly for a particular child or would wait too long and leave a parent feeling embarrassed that they had failed in some way. Over time we found out what worked well for the children:

- asking parents not to duck out without saying goodbye;

- parents and family workers being firm and kind with the child who they think is ready for a short amount of time unaccompanied;

- parents being consistent about coming back at the agreed time.

Italian nursery workers are very clear that they are not surrogate mothers or 'mothers made conscious' (Steedman, 1988). They encourage the children in their nurseries to take emotional support from their peer group. We found however, that children needed a special person to offer lots of touch and cuddles during the transition from home to nursery. Sometimes the family worker would need to sit close by and just be with a child if he or she could not immediately be comforted.

Considering children's feelings

This way of settling the children certainly increases the stress for members of staff. Nursery workers are most exposed to the public eye during these transition times. Perhaps parents and early-years educators cannot be blamed for taking the view that it's best to get it over with . . . but best for whom?

> *The power relations between adults and children are all wrong . . . they must be changed so adults would no longer be convinced of their right . . . to arrange the life and world of the child as* they *think best, without considering the child's feelings about it.*
> (Korczak in Bettelheim, 1990)

However painful or protracted, the transition from home to nursery needs to be handled respectfully.

Pen Green's admissions policy

Our admissions' criteria were inevitably driven by our two principal funding agencies, the Education and Social Services Departments. The assumption had been made by the steering group that nursery places would be allocated equally to 'children in need' and to children in need of a nursery place – a subtle distinction! Rigid criteria have never been adopted.

Many of the family centres, day nurseries and voluntary sector provisions which we visited were required by their funding bodies to establish formal written guidance on admissions. Often their criteria revolved around whether children were seen to be 'at risk' or were already on the NSPCC Child Protection Register. Other criteria commonly used for allocating places included whether the children had emotional or behavioural problems; whether the child had a developmental delay or whether the parent was a single parent.

It seemed that decisions about offering children places were value-based depending on the kind of priorities which particular funding agencies and staff groups in particular parts of the country chose to adopt. In many instances day-care admissions in England are based on the availability of day-nursery places rather than the expressed or apparent needs of children and families (Bone, 1977, Moss, 1984). A child might well qualify for a priority day-nursery place in one part of the country who would have spent years on a waiting-list in another.

In the local education authority nursery units and schools and in the combined centres we visited, admissions' criteria were also laid down and some children were referred by health visitors or social workers against these criteria. Others were admitted when their names came up on a waiting-list. Clearly only the best-informed and most organised parents would get their children's names down on the waiting-list at the appropriate time. Although *in theory* nursery education was available to all children equally, in practice, less articulate, less informed families were discriminated against (Osborn and Milbank, 1987). Parents at Pen Green used to call it the 'You have to bang your child on the head to get him a nursery place syndrome!' because, having failed to secure a legitimate place on the waiting-list at the right time, they had to resort to illigitimate means.

Initially we felt our catchment area would in itself be a limiting factor. We wanted to discover in practice what the demands and needs of our local community were. Since there was no reliable, up-to-date information on the numbers of children under-five in the area, we simply had to wait and see.

A flexible approach to admissions

With the kinds of grass-roots pressure for places that all our local under-eights provisions have been experiencing recently, it is possible to look back and see how privileged we were to have little of the departmental pressure experienced elsewhere. Staff and parents were given a great deal of space to define how the nursery would work and this definition needed to be organic since socio-economic factors in the community were constantly changing – as were the needs of our nursery population.

The Labour administration in the County Council gave both officer and member support for our policy of being responsive to *all* families with young children in the local neighbourhood. Political and practical constraints (in the form of huge waiting-lists, and enormous pressure on us to take 'referred' children) have made it impossible for us to retain a completely open-door policy but the *principle* of making under-fives provision available to all who wanted it in one form or another has driven our practice to this day.

If a nursery place was not immediately available that did not mean the door was closed to that child or parent. By the time we had been open a year, we were able, with the support of parents and link workers from health, social services and child and family guidance, to offer the children on our nursery waiting-list a place in the playgroup or in a play session for parents with children under three. This had implications for our role as 'professional', that is paid, staff since we were not the only providers of services. It led to a complex and exciting partnership between paid staff and volunteers. Many volunteers have subsequently been able to earn a small amount as paid volunteers, running crèches, playgroups and adult-education groups. As a baseline we established the principle that *any* child could use the centre at almost any time during the week if their parent was prepared to stay with them. (Again it was our spacious, non-purpose-built building which made this possible.)

At the same time we made the radical decision to offer a community morning every Wednesday geared towards children on the waiting-list, childminders, foster parents and, particularly, parents with special needs children who often travelled in from outlying villages and even from the neighbouring county of Leicestershire.

Opening the nursery door

Our first priority was to make sure the nursery was used fully. Applications came from families with a variety of wants and needs on a 'first come, first served' basis. We were desperate to get going and opened at the end of the summer term – the day the architects and builders finally moved out.

We took everyone who wanted a place, even children who were going up to primary school at the end of the summer, just so that they would have a taster experience of nursery during the summer holidays. We met, for the first time, parents of children with special needs who were having to face a whole seven weeks with no play schemes or respite care. These were parents whose children were taken by bus to a neighbouring town from eight o'clock to four o'clock each day during term-time.

In our first written report in September 1983 (only two months after opening) we wrote:

> We firmly wish to maintain a balance between providing straightforward pre-school provision for some children, while at the same time relieving the burdens and strains which some families are undergoing, either permanently or temporarily.

Analysing need: a market research approach to admissions

In a way, our admissions' policy mirrors our whole approach to working with children. Firstly:

- *observe* and *understand* the context within which children and family are living;

- *listen* to, and get feedback from them about *what they want* and then plan accordingly; and

- if at all possible *extend* what is available.

After only ten weeks we were able to show that:

- fifty-seven children were attending the nursery (plus older and younger siblings on an informal basis);

- the greatest unmet demand was for two to three-year-olds for whom there was no other local authority provision available;

- twenty children had been referred by social services, health visitors or the probation services.

- by trying to replace 'no' with 'maybe', we can find a way around this problem of too many children and too few places. Alternative services were established at the same time as our nursery grew.

With the parents' permission we analysed the stress factors which they were experiencing in their domestic situations (Bone, 1977). Using this research, we were able to make the point to both of our funding agencies that seven of the families experiencing the greatest difficulties (by their own definition and using the DHSS criteria) had just walked into the nursery; they had not been referred and were not currently receiving any support from statutory agencies. It seemed, in 1983, that a number of the families most urgently requiring the support the welfare state was set up to provide were actually slipping through the net. A more careful analysis of our nursery intake for 1989 to 1990 shows that seventy-two per cent of the children and their families using the nursery in that year required additional (not specifically educational) support. This support included welfare rights; housing advice; counselling; family therapy; support when experiencing difficulties with their child's behaviour; health advice for parents or children, financial support through emergency 'poverty payments' and a variety of other kinds of help.

The value of our policy
There is a stunning photograph on a wall in the centre taken in 1984 of three four-year-old girls who just by chance, had sat down together on the front

steps. They are wearing hats and carrying handbags and one even has a discarded cigarette butt in her mouth. This photograph emphasised for us the importance of maintaining as open an admissions' policy as possible. One child had been in and out of care several times and the only really consistent person in her life, who had time to show her love and affection, was her family worker. Another had chronic asthma and the third was a gentle child who was sometimes bullied. All three, we felt, had a *right* to nursery education, all three had a *need* for it, and, with pressure on places, only one would have technically qualified for it.

CHOOSING OUR PATH — LOOKING FOR CONSENSUS AND SETTING BOUNDARIES

From the outset one of the hardest tasks we faced, as a multi-disciplinary staff group in which individuals held different belief systems and values, was to find common ground on what kind of boundaries we felt it important to establish with young children and what behaviour we wanted to encourage.

Traditionally, practitioners writing about early-years education and care seem to assume a high degree of staff consensus with regard to values about children and a shared belief system about how children learn. It is as if the only problem occurs when 'professional' views clash with the views of 'parents'. Our experience was that there were as many different views about the right way to love, comfort and educate a young child as there were members of staff. Of course, part of the problem may have been that we positively recruited a staff group with strong opinions, which is *not* the same thing as an opinionated staff group.

Some writers seem to present nurseries as 'value-free' establishments as if the almost inevitably all-female role models offered to children, the often narrowly drawn up admissions policy, and the rigid boundary-setting in terms of children's hours and attendance were not all culturally determined and value based. Obviously in the nineteen nineties some nursery staff groups do discuss these issues and are being encouraged to do so by using new materials designed for workers in the education and day-care sectors (Drummond, Rouse and Pugh, 1992). However, in 1983, we had had few opportunities for 'cultural defamiliarisation' (Tobin, 1989).

It was not until staff visited nurseries in Denmark and Italy in 1991 and

1992 that we realised just how much of what we had taken for granted was culturally determined. When we shared seminars with colleagues who had visited early-years provisions in Japan and Romania and had trained staff in other parts of Europe, and when we had worked much more closely with parents from minority ethnic groups, we really appreciated that there was more than one way of educating, nurturing and showing love to a child. Priorities about young children's education are not necessarily based on universally held norms about what's 'good' for children (Tobin, 1989, p. 198) but are also linked to socio-economic and political factors.

Establishing common ground

Those first few months before the centre opened gave us the opportunity to challenge, question and establish what were commonly held principles and practice. Some staff wanted children to have unlimited, uninterrupted time to play and use the nursery provision; others felt that children needed more guidance and direction and that morning and afternoon sessions could be divided up to include a family group time when children would meet in their small groups. We tried to determine whether decisions about the organisation of the nursery were made because they were good for children or because they were good for staff. Compromises often have to be made in the nursery day because of practical constraints but it seemed important not to make a virtue out of a necessity. (For example, in our nursery, children *have* to sit together in a group for a few minutes before walking over for lunch because some staff need to go off and take their breaks and other staff arrive to eat with the children.)

We were an individualistic staff group: each with strong views and we enjoyed expressing them. What we wanted to provide for children was also what we wanted for ourselves: an environment where questioning and challenging were encouraged; where people were encouraged to plan, make decisions and find support in carrying them out; where they experienced success, or enjoyed learning and making mistakes (Moyles, 1989, p. 27). We felt this last experience was so important that we cited one such example in our curriculum document:

> *Children were fetching water from the bathroom to fill a large baby bath tub. One child failed to return with her container full, and was overheard in the bathroom expressing concern that her large sieve just wouldn't fill up!*

Whose choice? – Working with children's anger

The powerful statement in our curriculum document (page 26) about children needing to 'feel strong, in control, able to question and able to choose' best expresses the consensus which we came to; boundaries *were* important and most children needed the security of a routine which included warm, intimate times with their family worker. Their family worker also took on the key role in dealing with conflict situations between children since we felt it was vital that children should get a consistent response from an adult with whom they had a loving relationship. Although other family workers would try and intervene at difficult moments, such as when one angry child bit another, or behaved destructively, the child's family worker would then take 'time out' to try and work through the problem. This might involve simply sitting close by so that in her anger the child should not feel abandoned.

> *The amount of destructiveness in a child is proportionate to the amounts to which the expansiveness of his life has been curtailed. Destructiveness is the outcome of the unlived life.*
> (Erich Fromm, 1963)

The theme of finding sensitive ways of working with angry children is one that has re-occurred in the last nine years. We have learnt that acknowledging a child's anger and pain is the starting point and telling him or her how you feel about what he's done is also helpful as long as it's within a framework of, 'I really like *you* and I *don't like* what you just did to . . . and I don't *want* you to do that again'.

Encouraging children to stay in touch with their anger and frustration and to release these feelings more creatively became a nursery goal. (This was achieved in part when we set up a safe, soft, bouncy, play therapy room.) We've spent a great deal of time finding ways to help children develop new non-aggressive strategies to make adults and other children listen to them and to feel heard. Conversely, we've worked hard with the victims – the shy gentle child who is just standing by wailing – to augment their coping strategies and to encourage them to be more assertive. We wrote our own assertiveness programme for under-fives entitled *Learning to be Strong* in 1986.

Structuring or constraining choice

Children need to be allowed to plan, to be offered a variety of firsthand experiences and to be in charge of their own learning. We always believed learning should be 'in the hands of the pre-school child, not the adult' (Nutbrown and David, 1992) and did not see this as implying that our role as educators should be to sit back and let them get on with it.

What we saw on many of our visits to other nurseries was that classroom organisation often denied children the right to feel in control or to follow their own interests. We observed a great deal of 'sitting on the mat' time, either for registration or in order that children might be directed to an activity where he or she would then be allowed to 'play freely'. We grew used to observing the 'five different choices in a morning syndrome' where children were moved around in groups from area to area or sometimes from day to day (that is, from wet area one day, to creative area the next). We also saw many rooms decorated with templates and a multiplicity of daffodils for Mother's Day and snowmen at Christmas. We saw nurseries where an appropriate drawing or a photograph would even be pinned up on the easel to make it easier for a child to 'get it right'.

Some of this may sound overstated in 1994. These observations were, after all made nine years ago, but they made a deep impression. We grew to dread the words 'structured play' because what we saw was a lot of teacher-imposed structure and not a lot of very imaginative or developed play. In the plethora of writing today on the early-years curriculum, considerable attention has been given to the dangers of the 'transmission approach'. Margaret Lally links this fairly closed view of how children learn with the need some teachers have to feel powerful, in control and to have a clear role (Lally, 1991, pp. 126–7).

Twenty-four years earlier, John Holt wrote that some teachers:

> Like to feel that they are at every moment in control, not only of the child's body but also of his mind. They like to feel themselves the source and the sole source of all knowledge, wisdom and learning in the classroom. Some such teachers are moved by a love of power, of which the classroom gives them plenty; others, by a deep and sometimes desperate need to feel useful, necessary, and even indispensable to their students. Both kinds are strongly threatened by any suggestion that children can and should learn on their own.

He goes on to make the point that many teachers are afraid that they and their pupils will be found wanting in standardised texts (Holt, 1967, pp. 145–6). Perhaps this fear is also shared by early-years educators in the nineties who are now confronted with the pressures of base-line assessments for four-year-olds and teaching *to* Attainment Targets.

In other early-years environments which we visited, and these included nursery units, social services day nurseries or family centres we observed a *laissez-faire* approach. Workers in these centres described their approach as 'child-centred' (Athey, 1990, pp. 24–5) but it appeared to us to be fairly lacking in cognitive challenge (David, 1990).

In those early days we heard a great deal of rhetoric about free play and children making decisions; and what we saw in practice was either a fairly didactic approach or alternatively a 'hands-off' approach. With hindsight and by learning through experience, we can see that we often failed to understand what was going on *in our own nursery* and lacked the 'professional vocabulary' (Athey, 1990; Drummond, 1989) to describe what we saw the children doing. We always tried, however, to honour children's emotional and cognitive processes for like Ghedini we believed that:

> . . . *there is no learning without an effective and emotional closeness to and involvement with, what we are learning, in a context where one is both captivated and somewhat attached to what is being learned.*
> (Ghedini, 1991)

Our nursery pedagogy

Creating a learning environment

> *Only an education which takes very seriously the child's view of things can change the world for the better.*
> (Janusz Korczak, 1990)

We translated our principles into practice by setting up an environment where children could undertake a lot of independent learning with firsthand experiences. The appearance of the nursery was probably not that different from many others, with conventional table-top toys, graded jigsaws, threading and matching games and a lot more plastic about than we would accept today. The difference lay in how the children made choices and were encouraged to use their time. Once again the enormous amount of space encouraged us to be inventive.

The room was divided up into bays, making what was offered appealing to children. We probably adopted a more homely nursery environment than many we had visited to compensate for the institutional nature of our building. Tables tended to be covered with **warm, rich** fabrics. Materials for painting, drawing and clay work were laid out in as inviting a way as possible; paper was put on boards on the floor, on easels, or on the wall; delicate brushes and delicate paint boxes with richer paper were also available. Carefully chosen books were arranged in baskets and boxes in all parts of the nursery, down the corridors and in our office and reception area.

Figure 6   Young children enjoying books

Books to borrow were put at both entrances and we also had, for several years, our own nursery community bookshop. The nursery children loved to have book club 'savings cards' where they paid as much as they could until half the price of the book was covered, and could then take it home and continue paying it off over time.

Display

We felt it was hugely important to create a warm, welcoming and visually exciting environment. The curtains and carpets were chosen by children so that we ended up with a riot of colour which cheered up all the adults. (We now also have rooms with quiet and subdued colouring and few distractions, which are used by children, staff and parents.)

Even in the early eighties our displays were fairly unconventional, as they tended to be of the 'climb up and do' and 'touch or eat' variety. These were intermixed with purely aesthetic displays of beautifully mounted children's work and nicely arranged flowers or whatever was seasonal. Some displays started with what the children brought in from home, or as a result of the nursery children's trips out.

Planning for children

In our 'definitive' report of September 1983 (as we then called it), we outlined for officers and members the way in which we planned for children.

> *The educational input is planned on two levels. Linked themes of work are planned ten to twelve weeks ahead and a member of staff allocated a theme, so that the planning and collecting of materials for that theme can take place over a period of weeks. Specific activities for the theme are chosen by the family workers and then discussed as a group at our weekly staff session. Each member of staff then takes responsibility to carry out a special activity each day, connected to the theme. For example, the themes for the coming weeks are – growing; size; shape; animals in autumn; autumn colours; animals in the centre; stirrings of winter; weird and wonderful (Halloween); and fire (bonfire night). The children will dig for worms and collect assorted mini-beasts which will be displayed, observed and cared for by the children.*

Our aim was to provide a wide range of interesting experiences for children and to encourage all staff to contribute to the planning and the preparation whether they were teacher-trained, had the NNEB qualification or had a background in social work. We were concerned that we were making an appropriately differentiated provision for the youngest child who at that time was eight months old, and for the two-, three- and four-year-olds. At this point we were still accepting social work referrals for children under eighteen months, although we realised fairly quickly that we could not provide the kind of consistent one-to-one staffing which a baby needs. We also found that in many cases non-working mothers preferred a short break from their very-young children, rather than having their low self-esteem confirmed by the removal of their child for extended periods of time.

We used the three-and-a-half hours' staff meeting on Wednesday afternoons to 'brainstorm' our ideas on to a planning sheet. This planning sheet highlighted all the areas of the curriculum that needed to be covered so that we could offer a suitably balanced provision. The exact headings we used were, creativity; construction; water dough; language/story; natural science; outings; imaginative activities and outside play. Somehow technology, science and maths always seemed to have to be added on.

Looking back it's possible to see how we tried to be very responsive to the children's expressed interests. Planned themes did not preclude spontaneous work being explored when children brought objects into the centre. For instance a child brought some treasured pebbles in and these were varnished, displayed and admired by the other children.

Using the outdoors creatively in a hostile environment

We worked hard to create an outdoor play provision which was a rich learning environment. This included tobogganing in the snow, using the parachute on windy days and having quantities of paddling pools and hosepipes when the sun was hot. The area consisted of grassed areas, trees and shrubs, which were ideal for den-building and secret retreats. Large cardboard boxes, hundreds of plastic milk crates (borrowed from the dairy) and large climbing equipment which could be draped or 'added to' were also generally put out each day. Some children wanted to spend most of their day outside at first, others preferred the warmth and excitement inside.

> *Given this freedom to choose, children do learn to negotiate their own day and develop their own rhythm.*
> (Pen Green *Curriculum Document*, 1985)

Outings

We spent a great deal of time widening children's experiences through regular outings. Going out in a minibus which we borrowed from the social services two days a week was the highlight of the week for some children (we got our own nursery minibus in 1985). All staff who were drivers made sure that their insurance covered carrying children and parents, and took small groups to visit farm parks; the woods; the local bakery; the fire station; local manor houses and even a hole in the road!

One of our most exciting trips was when parents, children and staff (including our assistant caretaker who was a brilliant photographer) took a train ride on an inter-city 125 from the neighbouring town of Kettering. The children had an early start with their snacks packed up in a small suitcase. They were picked up by the minibus at the next station and drove back through country lanes where they saw new-born lambs. This led to a month-long exploration of wool, weaving, dyeing wool and cloth. One member of staff regularly adopted a rejected or orphaned lamb and kept it for a short time in a cardboard box in her office where it was well-loved and fed regularly, with total fascination by the nursery children.

Other trips simply involved walking down the road. One December the children wrote letters to Father Christmas, asked our secretary for stamps, wrapped up warm, and walked to the post office to post the letters. On the

Figure 7   One of our most exciting day trips from the nursery

children's return from their short Christmas break a reply awaited them from the London post office's Father Christmas! Sometimes family workers might take children and parents to their own homes for tea and biscuits, or to the local community bookshop, where hot chocolate was a special treat in winter.

We became increasingly aware that the themes which we spent so much time elaborating in staff meetings and building-up as a staff group, were largely irrelevant to the nursery children. They played on despite us. We had identified and planned around particular themes so as to offer the children appropriate curriculum content; themes had proved to be a very useful focus for all our ideas and energy. In the future we were to focus much more on the processes by which individual children were coming to an understanding of their world. We observed children experimenting with and learning to control their environment, and devoted our energies to making that environment rich and inviting.

An anti-bias approach: combating racism and gender stereotyping

The staff at Pen Green had some awareness of race issues and many of us had previously enjoyed working in multi-cultural settings. It seemed strange to be in a town with an almost exclusively white population. We worked hard at developing anti-racist strategies in the nursery; it has been a real challenge to staff to support and extend children's learning about ethnicity when there are so few minority ethnic groups in Corby and in the nursery children's own life experience.

In the beginning we had only one child from a minority ethnic group in the nursery, and in some years there were no children from minority ethnic groups on the waiting-list at all. We looked to colleagues in London for advice and took our four-year-olds to London to a Greater London Council (GLC) Fun Day where some staff joined in the fun with the children and some attended seminars on anti-racism. We then borrowed a number of wonderful home-corner 'treasure chests' and set up an Aladdin's Cave of clothes, kitchen utensils and toys from many different countries and cultures, in the neighbouring former school hall.

We invited colleagues from other schools and nurseries and set up a number of workshops for parents and staff on race awareness. Our efforts were not always well received. Some parents and teachers saw it as inappropriate. One visiting head teacher commented on how self-conscious it all was: 'We don't have a race problem in Corby.' Our own experience was that the four-year-old Asian child in our nursery was already feeling so vulnerable that he was giving the other children sweets to ensure their friendship and that some nursery children would refuse to hold hands with him. One way round this mono-culturalism was to introduce the idea of celebrating differences in both the nursery and the family room. This involved fireworks, steel bands and wonderful food, all of which proved popular. When an all-white busload of Corby children, parents and family workers attended a Diwali street festival in Leicester it was probably their first real experience of our multi-cultural society; an experience heightened by finding themselves for once in the minority. Derman-Sparks (1989, p. 7) points out the dangers of focusing on festivals and holidays as 'added-on' components of an early years curriculum. We have always provided a visually rich environment where photographs, games and toys reflect cultural diversity. We also have displays of photographs which celebrate the fact that some of the nursery children have either a parent, brother, sister, or grandparent with a different ethnic origin and culture.

We have gained confidence in working on our own attitudes and in tackling racism more directly as it occurs (Iram Siraj-Blatchford, p. 119.) We had always done this with the nursery children but had found it harder to approach their parents.

Staff were encouraged to look long and hard at their attitudes towards gender. As we were an all-female staff group we tried to encourage men on community care courses at the local college to help in the nursery, and we had several male volunteers through college placements or through employment schemes. We worked hard with parents on issues like allowing the boys in the nursery freedom to walk around in tutus, high heels and handbags, and to use the dressing-up clothes, prams, dolls and home-corner as they wanted to. We positively encouraged girls to use the construction equipment, the woodwork table and the computer and they too had their play protected. We introduced books which contained stories with positive images of girls and boys purchased from shops like Sisterwrite in London.

Parents were often amused by our endeavours and sometimes not so amused. None of the staff who were there will forget one Christmas party when Father Christmas presented a four-year-old boy with a picnic set which was what he'd really wanted. His mother threw it to the ground and stormed out with him in anger and distress. We grew to realise that it was unhelpful to move things too fast. Home values and nursery values both had to be respected. It was not helpful for children if they were so crudely exposed as different. If we were to challenge such fundamental precepts in society then we needed to make sure that parents shared our views. On some occasions we had to accept that changes would only happen over years, not over a few short months, and that any kind of change can be threatening. Ted Hughes' poem again seems wonderfully relevant.

A little at a time, of each new thing is best,
Too much and too sudden is too frightening.
(Ted Hughes, 1976)

Negotiating with parents our approach to children

Exchanging information: what do staff, parents and children want?

At Pen Green we presented both our nursery programme and our beliefs about how children learn most effectively through our curriculum document for parents. Good relationships with parents were built up through showing parents round the centre on their initial visit and by visiting their children at home. These visits gave family workers the opportunity to learn about a child's special words, their loved objects, their friends and how and where they liked to play at home. Home visits also gave parents the opportunity to outline their anxieties and their hopes. Throughout the first few years we ran a course on Understanding nursery education and parents on this course gave us their views on what was important to them. Parents at Pen Green placed most emphasis on children developing social skills. We had comments such as:

My child is clingy, nursery school is getting her ready to trust other people.

Learning to share, a little independence and playing with bigger children.

Pen Green parents are not alone in seeing socialisation as a priority. Seventy per cent of Japanese parents chose 'to give children a chance to play with other children' as one of their top three answers to the question 'Why should a society have pre-schools?' (Tobin and Davidson, 1989).

We explained to the parents that they could negotiate with us the hours their child needed in the nursery on our first home-visit. Some children started at half-past eight in the morning (or sometimes earlier if a parent was on an early shift) and went home at half-past three; some came for just a morning session from nine o'clock until mid-day; some stayed to lunch; some came only in the afternoon. These hours could be re-negotiated if family circumstances changed: the arrival of a new baby, a child still needing a nap at a specific time, or a change of parent's working hours. As the years went by, pressure for places increased and it was not possible to be as flexible as we would have liked. The *principle* of flexibility, however, remained.

How children spend their time

During their time in nursery, parents saw that the children were encouraged to make decisions about what they wanted to do from all the different experiences that were on offer. Some children chose to spend all their time outside, some were very active and then spent quiet times sitting on someone's lap and having a story read to them. Children spent most of their time exploring the environment through physical experiences by:

> *running; jumping; climbing; dancing; through feeling and experimenting with clay; paints; sand and water; by touching, smelling and tasting things around them. They experience themselves in relation to the world and learn to respect and enjoy the environment. We encourage their insatiable curiosity and sense of awe and wonderment at what they find.*
> (Pen Green *Curriculum Document*, 1985)

Encouraging self-esteem

We emphasised to parents the importance we placed on the development of self-esteem. We talked to them about children's need for positive affirmation through taking paintings and drawings home or having them displayed at the nursery. Even in 1983 we often used photographs as a record of the children's achievements and these have become increasingly important. A sequence of photographs can often show a child's intense concentration and creativity much more clearly than the products of her labour. We made a collection of children's books which dealt honestly with children's feelings of pain, anger, bewilderment and sense of loss and we used these and encouraged parents to borrow them, if their child was troubled in any way. Children also told us stories about the things they were excited about, or what they were feeling and their words were made into books, sometimes with photos or pictures.

Emphasising process not product

We constantly reassured parents that it was the process and not the end result that was important. We needed to work hard to win parental support as the children were sometimes either late back from a trip or wet and dirty by the end of a session. (Our washing machine and tumble-dryer were constantly in use and parents knew they could use these facilities if they needed to.) Some parents found it hard to accept the children's fascination with banging and moulding clay, dough or blocks of ice, feeling slimy spaghetti in water or the feel of thick finger-paints on a shiny surface. We sometimes introduced a practical element into our Understanding nursery education course so that they could get in touch with the pleasure of playing with such materials. Some parents became fairly tolerant while remaining unconvinced.

We also outlined to parents the extended periods of time young children needed to learn rules and build concepts. This could be achieved by playing with wooden bricks or building with blocks; by racing cars down a ramp or by riding tricycles through a wall of wooden blocks; or by asking questions and reflecting on things that had happened. Parents needed to know that children were being encouraged to take things apart, sometimes literally, by dissecting a fish, taking a clock to pieces, plucking a pheasant, or by taking things apart intellectually.

Children's profiles — observing and assessing

The way in which staff approached their assessments of the children's development best indicates the enormous value which we placed on the information provided by parents about their children and how much we needed that information if the nursery was to provide a rich experience for their child. At this stage (1983–5) we were primarily concerned with the social, the emotional and the linguistic needs of children. Like Tizard and her colleagues we felt:

> it is time to shift the emphasis away from what parents should learn from professionals and towards what professionals can learn from studying parents and children at home.
> (Tizard, 1984, p. 267)

Each family worker was responsible for keeping a file for each child in her family group. It was important that all these files were openly accessible to parents. This was true even if the child had been referred by social services so that all children were seen to be treated in the same way. Case notes on children and letters from other statutory agencies were filed separately in locked cabinets in another room to ensure confidentiality, whereas all the children's nursery files were kept in the front reception area where they were easily available to parents. Parents would also have a chance to see them on home visits. We had a centre policy, long before it became accepted practice in the local authority, to only write or record information we were prepared to share with parents. Although at times this was hard for staff and certain things were painful for parents to read, it seemed an important principle. We were not at liberty, however, to share information from other professional colleagues and felt concerned that, despite the Data Protection Act, parents still did not have an automatic right to access everything that was written about them or their children.

First home-visit

After her first home-visit, the family worker noted the child's special interests, toys or rituals. She would record how the child had settled into nursery and reacted to being away from her parents and she would write about the child's developing friendships and how she related to adults in the nursery; about the things she seemed to most enjoy and any times she found particularly difficult.

After about three months, each family worker made another home-visit at a time which suited the family, to talk to the parents. This was an opportunity to look at each child's development in some detail, with the parents and family worker both filling in the form.

Sometimes the parents made a major contribution to this developmental assessment. Sometimes it was the family worker who did most of the recording. We recognised the fact that children were often very different at home and we wanted to hear the parents' views about how things were going, and to share our concerns and our plans. Family workers generally built up an understanding of each child's development through observation sheets filled in by all the staff.

Observations in the nursery

These observations could be of an interaction between children; an extended piece of conversation overheard in the home-corner; a newly acquired skill; or something which had delighted and captured the child's imagination. There were occasions when family workers were concerned about a child, or were unclear about how a particular child was 'using' the nursery. Then, with the parents' consent, we would make a detailed study of that child over a few days. This involved everyone carrying notebooks and making sure they recorded in detail everything they saw that child involved in; who with; for how long; and the conversation itself, if at all possible.

These 'child studies' make fascinating reading, especially with our increased knowledge of repeated patterns in children's play. We were concerned sometimes about children apparently flitting from one activity to another (Athey, 1990). Sometimes we felt we were not understanding their current obsession, even though we listened to both the children and their parents.

Children may appear 'off target'

Stephen was a child about whom we had this kind of anxiety. He was a child who seemed fairly immature in his use of language and who constantly seemed to race around the nursery with an object stuck down his jumper. He started off by using a sword that he had brought from home, which we banned (no swords or guns in the nursery was one of our four rules), and which he determinedly replaced with a stick, a ruler or a plastic tube. Our impression was that he was always on the run, living a very exciting, fantasy life with his 'weapon'. After a week's observation we came to realise that we had only been noticing his noisy behaviour and not the times when he was settled. He was in the nursery on a full-time basis and was in fact making good use of the environment. We also realised that he was using the 'He-Man' character, a legendary children's television favourite, about whom most of us knew very little.

Studying the patterns in children's play

Our concern in those early days was with the content of what Stephen was doing and whether it was worthwhile in terms of the early-years curriculum that we were offering. We did not have a readily available vocabulary to describe his play or to identify the 'cognitive forms', the 'schemas' which were *his* central concern. Chris Athey and Tina Bruce in the Froebel Early Education Project (Athey, 1990; Bruce, 1987; 1991) identified and studied the repeated patterns in young children's play and the schemas of children's thinking. Today, having had in-service training and three years of 'schema-spotting' in the nursery, we can see that Stephen's dominant schema was a concern with 'dynamic trajectories'.

> Trajectory
> *A fascination with things moving or flying through the air e.g. balls, aeroplanes, rockets, catapults, frisbees, and indeed, anything that can be thrown. When*

expressed through own body movements this often becomes large arm and leg movements, kicking and punching, etc.
(Nicholls [ed.], 1986)

At that time we just didn't have sufficient awareness or understanding to extend Stephen's thinking with 'worthwhile curriculum content' (Athey, 1990). We couldn't 'feed his schemas' in the way that we would if he were in the nursery today. We can be proud however that, although we didn't understand his behaviour, our first thought was not to thwart it but to understand it better by close observation.

> *The reflective practitioner . . . sees her role as fostering construction on the part of the child, as opposed to instruction by herself, and developing autonomy and co-operation, rather than using coercion and demanding obedience.*
> (David, 1990; also Drummond, 1993; and Paley, 1981)

We gave him opportunities to express himself without hurting or disturbing other children. Nursery staff took the time to watch his super-hero on television and then we set up a 'space-age' area with tunnels and a climbing frame and took him on walks with a small group of children to buy 'sherbert space sweets' (the kind which explode in your mouth) which were then shared with the rest of the children.

The observations that we made of Stephen led us to give him a lot more approbation for behaviour which had previously only been seen in rather negative terms. There seems to be a real paradox in the fact that the very experiences which come directly from children themselves always seem to be much messier, take more time, and are often apparently inconvenient to adults but provide possibilities for very rich learning. Those which are adult-directed and contained leave the nursery much tidier but the learning is fairly short-lived and fairly limited (the five activities in a morning syndrome, again). Educators have been saying this for a long time:

> *If education were defined, to include everything that children have learned since birth, everything that has come to them from living in the natural and the human world, then by any sensible measure what has come before five to six years-of-age would outweigh all the rest. When we narrow the scope of education to what goes on in schools, we throw out the method of that early and spectacular progress at our peril.*
> (Hawkins, 1965)

Parents were generally fascinated and pleased that we spent so much time recording what their children did, and using the approach outlined in figure 8 on page 61 we made the assessment process explicit to them. We realised early on that the development assessments we were using (of the checklist variety) were fairly simplistic and confusing for parents. A child might be given a developmental assessment at three years old by the health visitor, and on the same day the nursery staff might sit down with parents and children with a different developmental assessment. Children were growing and developing so fast that our summative assessments were generally out of date by the time they appeared in the child's file, and the kind of information which they gave us did not seem to lead naturally into our planning for children's play. Staff preferred making a collection of observations on the children in their family group, because these observations seemed much more dynamic and did link well with our daily planning for children's play.

The family worker's observations, as well as being shared with parents, were also used in supervision/support sessions which each family worker had with a senior member of staff. Family workers would bring their files to these sessions and use their observations to reflect on the children in their family group and to make decisions about what special provision 'their' children might need in the nursery. These ideas could then be brought back to the nursery staff meetings.

Most family workers enjoyed reflecting on the children verbally but, for some, writing about children's development in this way was agony. Many of the nursery staff had not enjoyed writing at college and some had experienced a real sense of failure in this area. There was never any suggestion, however, that only the teachers should record (a system we have come across in some nurseries).

Focus on parents

Parents are very important people.

> *Parents and professionals can help children separately or they can work together to the greater benefit of the children.*
> (Athey, 1990)

It must already be apparent from the amount of time we spent sharing

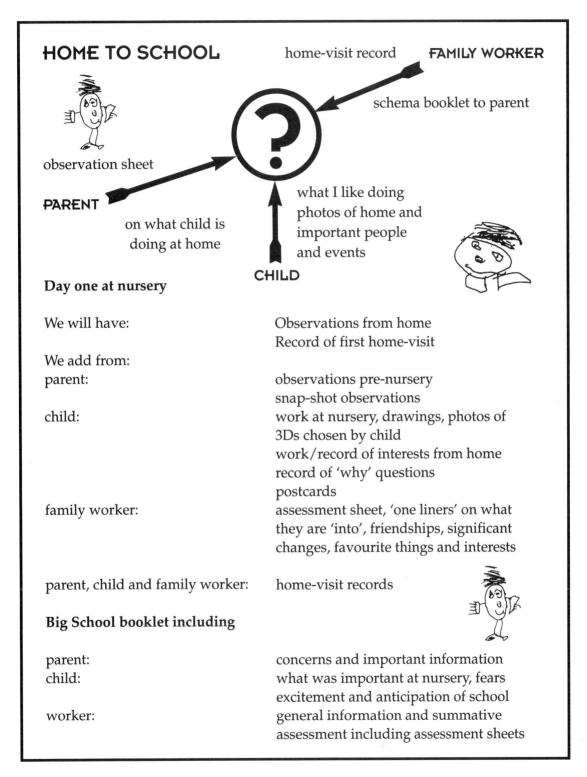

HOME TO SCHOOL   home-visit record   **FAMILY WORKER**

schema booklet to parent

observation sheet

PARENT

on what child is
doing at home

what I like doing
photos of home and
important people
and events

CHILD

Day one at nursery

We will have: Observations from home
                                       Record of first home-visit

We add from:
parent: observations pre-nursery
                                       snap-shot observations

child: work at nursery, drawings, photos of
                                       3Ds chosen by child
                                       work/record of interests from home
                                       record of 'why' questions
                                       postcards

family worker: assessment sheet, 'one liners' on what
                                       they are 'into', friendships, significant
                                       changes, favourite things and interests

parent, child and family worker: home-visit records

Big School booklet including

parent: concerns and important information
child: what was important at nursery, fears
                                       excitement and anticipation of school
worker: general information and summative
                                       assessment including assessment sheets

Figure 8   Introducing assessment to parents

information with, and asking for information from, parents that we saw their role as a vital one. As New Lodge Nursery in Belfast states:

> No other adult in the building can possibly know as much about this small new person as his parent does, and, in the beginning the teacher must depend on the parents' knowledge in helping the child to settle happily in the nursery school. (Department of Education for Northern Ireland, 1977)

Getting parents in to the nursery: parents and staff anxieties

Our first problem was getting parents to come in to the nursery. In our original advertisement for the centre we invited parents 'to stay as long as you want'. With very high unemployment and no other local resources for parents and children it seemed likely that some parents would spend a considerable amount of time at the centre and many did. We recognised the fact that for other parents the last place on earth they wanted to be was in the nursery, since with two or three children under five they were desperate for a respite from child-care.

A number of parents preferred to stay for the two-week settling-in period and then have a peaceful break at home, only returning to join in activities at the centre many months later. Some parents, and it has always been a minority, wanted to spend time in the nursery itself and really felt comfortable spending time with their children in that environment. These parents often said they found the family room cliquey and found it easier to make relationships with staff than with other parents.

We did not assume that because a parent chose not to stay at all or chose to do something for themselves rather than staying in the nursery, that they did not care about their child's development. Working alongside professionals can be very daunting for some parents, especially if the professionals also feel vulnerable about their own professionalism. Many of the staff initially felt inadequate with parents around. Parents expressed anxieties about whether their children would 'play up' if they stayed. Staff were worried that children wouldn't listen to them if the parents were present or that parents wouldn't approve of what they were doing. We've had to look constantly at these issues. Our first approach was to get parents and staff to 'brainstorm' how awful they felt and to step into each other's shoes. In those early days we spent a lot of in-service time examining how we kept parents out, albeit unconsciously.

In the same way, a few years later during in-service sessions, we looked at how we might be 'keeping male parents out' by either our behaviour or through the environment we were offering – which by then was very women- and children-friendly. In one office there used to be a long list of things identified by parents that discouraged them from coming into the nursery such as:

- there is no-one to look after your younger siblings;

- feeling that younger children aren't welcome;

- no-one to greet you or smile at you;

- no smoking.

All of these comments helped staff to reflect on how daunting institutions are to people 'on the outside'. We also had a list of things that parents had said helped them come into the nursery; it became a guide for good practice.

Our beliefs as a staff group about why it was a good thing to have parents in the nursery varied, but none of us ever subscribed to the view that parents were there to be educated to become more effective parents. Many of the parents who used the centre were surviving the difficult times and enjoying the good times in being a parent. For those parents that weren't, we didn't feel it was our role to teach parenting skills even if we could have clearly identified what they were. We didn't feel that loving, caring, negotiating, compromising and being consistent could come into the category of 'skills to be taught'! We have only come across a very small number of parents who actually did not know what to do in caring for their children. In one case a parent with learning difficulties, who had been in care herself since she was of nursery age, found it hard to care for her three-year-old appropriately. However, most of the parents using the nursery had a very good understanding of 'what you were supposed to do' with children. They had absorbed a great deal of information on the theory of child-development from Open University programmes on early morning television, often watched while nursing a restless baby to sleep, or because a toddler had decided the day would start at quarter past five in the morning.

Avoiding stereotyping parents

We were aware that parents tended to be put into no-win situations; that teachers, researchers and policy makers often had fairly negative feelings about what contribution parents could make in the nursery – and on whose terms (Tizard, Mortimore and Burchell, 1981; Athey, 1990). The Warnock Report (1978) stated that:

> Parents can be effective only if professionals take notice of what they say and how they express their needs and treat their contributions as intrinsically important.

Professional attitudes towards parents remained ambivalent, however, and Baroness Mary Warnock later described 'indifferent' parents as being 'less trouble'! (Warnock, 1985). It was clear to us that many of the compensatory programmes, set up in the sixties, had misrepresented what parents were actually doing at home and had stereotyped parents on class lines.

> a policy which is based on assumptions that certain parent cultures constitute a problem is not only grossly misleading but is positively unhelpful.
> (Docking, 1990)

Parents experiencing difficulties

Some parents were certainly finding the bringing up of their children neither easy nor pleasurable. There were parents who were choosing to repeat the patterns of how they had been parented: giving children few choices and in turn finding them very demanding. The first session of our Understanding nursery education course was almost always spent on getting parents to share with each other how they had been parented and whether they were using the same model with their own children.

A few parents were using physical punishment in a way which staff found unacceptable. The most depressing comment for us all, used by a parent to a crying child, was: 'What are you crying for? . . . I'll give you something to cry about!' – and this would be followed by a slap on the head or leg or whatever was nearest. Paradoxically we learnt from our Understanding nursery education course that a few parents who had experienced corporal punishment themselves at home and at infant and junior schools less than twenty years ago *still* felt that such treatment was appropriate. 'It never did me any harm' was another comment we grew to hate.

Some of the youngest parents had unrealistic expectations of what little children could give back. They felt let down when the relatively passive baby stage was followed by the challenge of a fast-moving two-year-old. There were always some parents who were overwhelmed by exhaustion, loneliness, marital conflict or mental health problems, and increasingly there were men and women trying to bring children up in poverty while living in hostels for the homeless.

In spite of their circumstances, most parents were desperately anxious to 'get it right' – particularly those families where children were on the Child Protection Register. We found that some parents were receiving input from as many as twenty professional workers, including community psychiatric nurses, clinical medical officers, education welfare officers, child and family guidance, social workers, NSPCC, the police, health visitors, teachers and so on. Each professional worker, inevitably, had a different view of what constituted the best way of bringing up a child! We quickly learnt that if a parent was feeling worried about an issue it was best to let them choose the person they wanted to turn to. Sometimes this was the family worker, sometimes another parent or a parent volunteer. If it were the family worker they wanted to talk to we would arrange for that member of staff to have time out of the nursery to be with a particular parent. This was seen as an important part of their nursery work (with huge implications for family workers' training.)

A balancing act

Staff saw their role as one which *complemented* that of the parent or parents. They did not want to compete with them or attempt to take over. Sometimes this presented the family worker with a conflict of interest: balancing the needs of a very young child for reassurance and cuddles and the needs of mothers who sometimes desperately wanted to escape from an overwhelming responsibility. The poem below, expresses this kind of stress.

The Unappreciated Wife

All day I do nothing but clean.
Yet it's hardly ever seen
To be tidy, or neat
I think I'll just seat
myself in a chair.

'Let it rot!'
Then see if we've got
Somebody who cares,
Other than me.

All day I do NOTHING but clean.
Yet they're hardly ever seen
Without chocolate, a wet nappy,
And I'm supposed to be happy
With a clothand some money
and hear someone say,
'Honey you do well'.
Wish I could yell,
'That's not for me!'

All day I do NOTHING but clean
And I'm seldom ever seen
As a woman, a person
Think I'll teach them a lesson
I'll just sit in a chair
'Let it Rot!'
We'll see if I've got
Somebody who cares
About ME!

(Sharon Hughes in *Reflections, Poetry by Pen Green parents, grandparents and staff,* 1985)

Tobin describes the dilemma of balancing parents' and childrens' needs:

> *Proponents as well as opponents of day care tend to share a commitment to the goals of life, liberty and the pursuit of happiness. The conflict lies in the question of* whose *life,* whose *liberty and* whose *happiness is to have priority.*
> (Tobin and Davidson, 1989, p. 178)

It was important, for instance, to address parents' practical difficulties such as the needs of a child's younger siblings in the nursery, or the need for flexibility in starting times if parents had some way to walk or if children (or parents) found it hard to get up in the morning. Once again, staff had to balance the needs of the children and the needs of the parents since it was obvious that for some children these changes in routine were fairly traumatic. Children who missed out on the gentle start to the day sometimes showed distress. It was, however, extremely difficult for some parents (for all sorts of reasons) to arrive at nursery at a regular time. Family workers needed to be as realistic and adaptable as possible and had to try to make time to greet the children individually even when they arrived halfway through the morning. On other occasions, family workers had to be advocates for the children and let the parents know things needed to change.

Parents and staff generally valued the relaxed settling-in time in the morning as a good time for exchanging news or voicing problems. Since children were arriving from eight-thirty in the morning, right through to ten or ten-thirty, it was much easier for family workers to take time with 'their' family group and to encourage children on an individual basis to get involved with whatever was happening in the nursery.

Parents in partnership with the centre

By 1985, parents were showing their interest in the nursery in a number of ways and most parents who were not working outside the home were involved. This was either in the form of voluntary work in the nursery or playgroup, running the toy library or nursery bookshop, fundraising, or speaking at conferences about the work of the centre. On many occasions both parents and staff departed in the minibus together for a conference; this cemented our partnership approach (Pugh, 1987).

Some might say that inviting parents to speak at conferences is a fairly tokenistic sort of partnership but these were parents who had *also* made their views felt within the centre. They had seen that things could change as a result of their views being expressed. Giving talks and making presentations also meant a lot to parents who felt they were being listened to by the professionals. For some it was a kind of 'role reversal', with parents on the podium for a change. This empowerment of parents was also experienced within the nursery through parents' meetings.

Parents' meetings and representation at Pen Green

Parents were actively encouraged to question what was going on in the nursery and a forum was set up to make this possible. A group of parents who used the centre met one evening a month; this was well attended during the first few years that the nursery was open. However, some of the parents who used these meetings said that it was hard to complain in a room full of strangers. They felt it was more important for them to meet the parents of the children in their child's family group since they would all have common concerns. We therefore set up alternative meetings called family group meetings during the day for which we provided crèche facilities. This also helped parents for whom evening meetings had become problematic because of changing employment patterns.

Both these meetings are very informal, rough minutes are taken and circulated to all the parents who haven't been able to attend so that they know which issues were raised and what was resolved.

Looking back at the minutes it is possible to see how different parents have used them in different ways. Some parents use them to air grievances or to challenge our nursery practice, some to ask for information or to make friends and get support.

Both the parents' monthly evening meeting and the family group meetings act as mechanisms of 'quality control' providing parents with an opportunity to give staff positive feedback and air grievances in an atmosphere of respect and warmth.

The parents of children in the nursery clearly did not hold one set of views about what constitutes a quality nursery experience for children. They cared principally about the happiness and development of their *own* child. These meetings therefore became a 'dynamic and continuous process of reconciling the emphasis of different interest groups' (Balaqueur, Mestres and Penn, 1992). The views of the nursery parents were then carried forward by parent-reps to the multi-disciplinary policy group which had overall responsibility for the centre.

In our experience most of the parents cared a great deal about their children's education, in part because their own experiences of schooling had been so painful. We tried to acknowledge the intensity of failure that some parents carried with them from their own school days and to work with parents' desire for something better for their children.

> *Education is opportunity, it is also a painful memory. To fail to understand the pain of past failures is also to fail to understand working-class life. It is essential then to combine both in your curriculum structure and pedagogy.*
> (Armstrong, 1986)

Not just tokenism

From the first moment that a parent fills in their application form, nursery staff at Pen Green encourage them to feel that they are welcome, and that the centre belongs to them. Reception areas are open and administrative staff are always available to respond to parents on a matter of paying dinner money or giving information about activities in the centre. Relationships with people always take priority over paperwork (Santos, 1992).

Perhaps parental involvement in a centre like Pen Green is about self-fulfilling prophesies. If staff have high expectations of parents' involvement in their children's education, either directly through daily contact in the nursery or indirectly through home-visits and evening meetings, parents will respond accordingly. Chris Athey includes parents' reflections on teacher expectations and self-fulfilling prophesies in her book *Extending Thought in Young Children*:

> *One mother had actively grasped the mechanisms of a self-fulfilling prophesy. In her child's school the parents were put in a hut in the playground and were asked to make things for the school jumble sale. With such trivial occupations there was some backbiting and parental drop-out. She noted humorously that the staff had taken this to be an instance of parent unreliability. She said she would be interested to see how many teachers would 'survive' the jumble-sale course.*
> (Athey, 1990, p. 63)

Staff at Pen Green shared the ideals of Mary Stacey whose work with parents at the Stroud Green Pre-School Centre in London, in the early eighties, left an incredible impression on those of us who had visited it. Like her, we set up the Pen Green nursery as 'a joint enterprise between parents and staff, with the goal of both being to further the child's development' (Stacey, 1991).

We were acutely aware, since we were both a social services and an education nursery, that so-called co-operation with parents could sometimes, in practice, be experienced as 'an iron fist in a velvet glove' – with parental involvement being 'required' rather than volunteered. Condry (1986) describes the failure of early-years workers to look at the hidden curriculum of control beneath the overt messages of co-operation in working with parents.

Because we were committed to a community-based approach there seemed to be no stigma attached to bringing children to the Pen Green nursery. As a staff group we did not accept that because some children were living in poverty and a minority were not having their needs met (either emotionally or physically) that this justified disempowering their parents.

In 1919, Margaret McMillan wrote:

> *. . . just as wealthier mothers employ nurses to care for their children, but do not give up responsibility or control, so this should also be the case in nursery schools*

. . . The existing nursery schools are not yet controlled by the mothers of the children who attend them. But already parent committees are being formed. (McMillan, 1919)

Years later we hope that we have succeeded in handing back some of that control to parents.

4 THE COMMUNITY NURSERY DEVELOPS 1985–92

A TIME OF RADICAL CHANGE

Dramatic changes were taking place in the streets around the centre. Housing, which had for a long time been left in a poor condition, was now sold off and young families were moving into the area. The shopping arcade was given a face-lift. Less positively, all the green spaces were soon covered in new housing developments and none of the developers provided public amenities or safe playgrounds for children. The community centre, which had housed several radical community action groups (including the local advisory group which had protested against the setting up of the nursery), also changed its brief. It closed down its youth facilities and became a community centre for services to the elderly, with funding from the Manpower Services Commission. This increased the frequency of angry reprisals throughout the estate by local teenagers.

Another major change occurred when a hostel for homeless families opened, a few streets away, where families lived in cramped accommodation, with a dining area shared by several families, no indoor or outside play facilities for children; and where adult lifestyles were constrained by evening curfews and marks awarded for rooms kept tidy! Many of the nursery's parents were still living on low incomes or were unwaged.

> *I used to help with the children . . . I used to stay all day, especially in the winter, because it saved on my bills as well. I used to come in the morning, put my son into the nursery and I would stay here. At three o'clock I would go home and light the fire up and I would come and get my son and the house would be nice and warm for him to go in.*
> (A nursery parent talking to Alaide Santos, 1992)

Changing lifestyles

Although the unemployment figures had dropped, from a nightmarish forty-three per cent in the 1980s to something nearer the national average (fifteen per cent in 1992), unemployment in Pen Green and neighbouring estates was still the highest in Corby and among the highest in the county. Those employed did not always find things easier since many parents worked twilight- or weekend-shifts which created huge problems for families in terms of after-school care. Some mothers were actually obliged to take children into the factories when they clocked on, to be handed over to fathers who were clocking off.

Another important change was that from 1983 to 1985 sometimes as many as two-thirds of the parents whose children used the centre were single parents. However, over the subsequent three to four years many of these single parent families became re-constituted families and the number of single parents dropped to less than a third of the families using the centre. At the same time, we began to get single parent fathers in the nursery.

The nursery was still serving a mainly white population, but a small number of children from minority ethnic groups also started to attend, along with children whose parents were from Latvia or the former Yugoslavia who did not speak English as a first language.

Admissions and new referrals

Our policy was still to admit children into the nursery from the age of two years but our long waiting-list meant that some local children would never get a place before they went to primary school. This meant that demands for other early-year provisions at the centre increased enormously. Our Wednesday morning community session was always full and the parent-run playgroup now ran every morning and afternoon. There was also a huge new demand for places for children under three in the nursery, both from statutory agencies who referred children to us and from parents in general. An increasing number of children with special needs were referred to the nursery and these were sometimes children as young as twenty months, for whom we had to make special one-to-one provision.

Internal changes to Pen Green's building

Both the community nursery and the centre as a whole had physically increased in size. We expanded into the neighbouring old comprehensive school building in 1985 (with the agreement of officers and the support of local councillors) and started to use rooms in two long corridors and the gymnasium. This meant that the nursery could set up a 'soft playroom' and had a much-increased outside play area and a gym for the youngest children's use. The playgroups could have their own space and an outside playground, which was also made available to an after-school club for five- to eleven-year-olds. These were our first nursery children who had now moved on to primary school and needed after-school facilities. The after-school club was run by parents and staff.

The large gym in the old comprehensive school was also now available for playschemes, and by this time there were playschemes every school holiday for children with special needs aged from three to eleven years. Playschemes for local children from five to eleven and eleven to eighteen years were also set up in the summer. These playschemes were run by paid staff, volunteers or the district council. The outside play spaces were once again made a priority and we set up a sonic playground with wonderful bell-towers and drums which proved very popular with children from the local Royal National Institute for the Blind school who came each week to share our space. In return the RNIB let us use their beautiful manor house and grounds on a weekly basis, and occasionally their bouncy castle and swimming-pool.

The most recent external changes occurred when we designed a new range of equipment for our nursery children which gave them increased opportunities to swing, climb, do circuits and slide. Additional space was also available for work which parent volunteers were heavily involved in, such as the setting up of a Children's Resource Centre (originally called the Scrap Project). This had started off as a small-scale project in a cupboard in the nursery and now expanded into the empty space to become a service for the whole county. Parent volunteers worked with one paid worker to create, with factory waste, a paradise for hard-up teachers, youth workers and playgroups. The resource centre was full of wonderful materials that every classroom needed and many useful materials that could not be bought from catalogues. Two large additional classrooms were also nicely decorated and set aside to be used by a number of parent groups.

The need for more staff

Labour lost control of the county council in 1985. We had successfully returned to the Education and Social Service committees in the first two years of the centre's life and had increased our nursery staff to nine full-time workers plus four part-time domestic staff and a secretary.

We tried to get additional funding for more staff to work with parents and secured six temporary posts, under a variety of Manpower Services Commission schemes. We wanted to achieve more stability for this work and so applied for Urban Aid Funding in 1985. This funding was for five years and meant that we had four new staff to work with parents and link-up with the schools and community. 1990 proved to be a fairly dramatic and painful year in the history of the centre, when we had to fight to secure the permanent funding of these posts through the County Council.

New staff come, and some original staff move on

The appointment of new staff brought many different kinds of expertise into the centre. For the first time we had men on the staff; this was to have a long-term impact on our nursery practice. There were also significant staff changes among our original 1983 staff groups, as family workers moved on to have babies or to continue their professional development.

Those of the original staff who were left had undertaken a great deal of training, and were able to work in a much more holistic way with the parents and children who used the nursery. They were also much more confident in working with colleagues from other agencies and by this time the list of other agencies involved in running services at Pen Green was comprehensive. Child and family guidance; social workers from children and family teams; mental health and disability services; health visitors and psychiatrists were all involved in running short-term or long-term groups for parents, either directly as co-leaders of groups, or indirectly by offering supervision to the staff who ran the groups. Educational psychologists; speech therapists; and the clinical medical officer all offered nursery staff and parents enormous amounts of practical support. Health visitors ran baby clinics, well-woman clinics, and gave family planning advice at the centre. Adult basic education, the Workers Education Association and adult education also ran groups or courses at the centre with, in many cases, ex-members of our own staff acting as tutors. Services for parents and children were running during the day, at twilight and in the evening.

CHANGES IN THE NURSERY PEDAGOGY: EVOLUTION AND CONSOLIDATION

Philosophy and practice evolve

By 1985, the nursery staff had evolved its philosophy of valuing autonomy in children and encouraging children to challenge and choose. Children came into the nursery having been visited at home several times and spent their first weeks in nursery with their care-giver or parent until they were ready to make a transition to their family group. Family workers, whatever their professional background, valued the link they had with parents and worked hard at creating a time for home-like routines and rituals and long periods of uninterrupted play in the nursery.

The children's emotional needs had to be paramount since children coming into the nursery sometimes seemed to be very angry or distressed. There is some evidence (Le Vine, 1983, p. 51; Tobin and Davidson, 1989, p. 198) that children born in low fertility cultures such as Britain's are given a lot of stimulation and little soothing, whereas in high fertility cultures children are soothed but are not given so much stimulation. The children who came into the Pen Green nursery certainly seemed to need intimate relationships with caring, consistent adults (Calder, 1990b; Honig, 1989). Increasingly, children were being referred who had been emotionally or physically abused and, although they were very much in the minority, their needs dominated the nursery at times.

Home-visiting – our philosophy is consolidated

As discussed in the last chapter, home-visiting gave staff a much clearer awareness of children's needs. For instance, Thomas was a two-and-a-half-year-old whose angry behaviour in the nursery could never have been understood without staff spending time at home with his family. The only two things Thomas had to play with during the first home-visit we made were an ashtray full of cigarette butts and a large Alsatian dog.

This dog accompanied him outside into an unfenced 'garden' where his Dad and Grandad were building and mending old cars. Thomas used very little language that we could understand in the nursery except for the few words he used to accompany his play. While throwing hollow wooden blocks into a heap he would say 'chuck' and then add a choice word from the vernacular, which rhymed with it beautifully! He would also throw furniture down the home-corner stairs, and when other children got involved, it became dangerous. A lot of his behaviour seemed undesirable and we needed to redirect his play rapidly so that he could make some positive relationships with staff and his peers and receive some praise.

At this stage we still weren't familiar with the work of Athey and Bruce but we watched Thomas and what we observed was a great deal of play which involved bonfire building and scattering and piling, reminiscent of what was going on in his own backyard. We encouraged him to build 'bonfires' outside with milk crates and wooden blocks; we took him on a trip to a car scrap-yard; we set up a car wash with crates and a petrol pump with old tubing. He was allowed to direct a hosepipe out through a nursery window; bin lids were hung-up from the trees in the nursery garden so that he could target them with bottles of water and gravel. In this way we tried to honour his most urgent

Figures 9 and 9a   Harnessing children's own interests ensures creativity and sustained effort

needs while at the same time encouraging him to enjoy gentler, more reflective times in the nursery.

Clearly not all of the children displayed such extreme behaviour as Thomas. Gradually our pre-occupation with children completing adult-initiated activities was replaced by a concern with how children were really learning.

New research: a philosophical home-coming

We were introduced to some wonderful new research at this time, when pedagogically we were somewhat in a vacuum. We had been focusing on responding to children and setting up provision that in some way equated with their current emotional and cognitive needs without always understanding where they were taking us. We saw some videos made by the Department of Education in Northern Ireland, accompanied by a small booklet entitled *Well Begun – theory into Practice in a Nursery School* and it seemed as if we had 'come home' philosophically speaking. We had attended seminars by Weikert in the early eighties, talked with colleagues who ran Headstart programmes and visited two 'High Scope Nurseries'. We had also attended courses and conferences where educators and psychologists expounded different theories of play and none of it seemed to fit with what was going on in our nursery. Perhaps it was because the work from Northern Ireland was very much practitioner research that it appealed to us, perhaps because the strife outside the nursery portrayed in the videos seemed to have some parallels with the strife going on in our nursery children's lives.

Guarding children's right to personal space and time

One of the key points we took from these videos was that children had a *right* to have their personal play protected. We saw a child building a tower and when other children tried to join in, the builder was asked by a member of staff if he wanted any one to help him, and he said 'No'. It seemed to make remarkable sense to us that those of our children for whom personal space was an unfamiliar concept, had the right to a bit of it in the nursery. No longer did we always interpret children not allowing others to join in, or even pushing them away, as reflecting anti-social behaviour. On the contrary a child's desire to finish a piece of work unaided was often a measure of her commitment to it.

Concomitant with this belief in children's right to independent play was the belief that children needed much longer periods of time to complete their pieces of work. It became increasingly important to record their achievements through photographs so that after several hours of undisturbed play the materials could be put away or someone else could begin to use them. Nursery sessions of two and a half to three hours just didn't work if they were constantly interrupted by snack times and group times. This meant that children in our nursery needed to be able to get to drinks and snacks at the time they wanted them and that the family group time, at its best a gentle reflective time, needed to be at the end of the children's busy morning.

The nursery as a workshop

The Northern Ireland videos confirmed our dissatisfaction with 'themes' which had long ceased to seem relevant to the children and which we had simply held on to as a crutch for us as a staff group. The focus in the nursery moved towards creating a workshop environment using all the most basic materials. For a few months, as an experiment, we threw out all external stimuli, like what was happening in the outside world, the seasons changing, input from trips out and so on, and focused instead on discovering the properties of clay, peat, water and sand. This proved to be an exhausting and exhilarating period for staff and children. It also led to real changes in our practice.

Much of the nursery had become a 'self-servicing' environment for children with crayons, paint and scrap materials all accessible at child-height. At times this was a nightmare – Thomas on the rampage could empty everything in minutes and our very youngest, least experienced children obviously didn't have the same sense of ordering and returning things as children who'd been in the nursery for some time. On the other hand, children were now mixing paints, choosing materials and taking much more control of their own learning.

It was with some relief, that after a few months, we allowed ourselves to celebrate outside events once again, and to once more use the outside world as a stimulus for what went on in the nursery. We had, however, learnt a lot about how children learn, by restricting ourselves for a short period to the most basic materials. Since these are the materials which are most readily available the world over, what we were observing was probably the kind of 'core' experimentation enjoyed by nursery-aged children in every culture.

Being strong

Our concern with children's emotional needs also led us to watch the withdrawn, vulnerable children in the nursery more carefully. We became more and more aware that these children had few strategies for coping with anger or hostility from their peers, (most just stood and wept, bereft of whatever they had been playing with). We also learnt a lot from the canny children who got what they wanted without a fight. At about this time (1989) parents expressed their concerns to us about the nursery children getting bullied when they left nursery and had to face the rigours of the big-school playground.

We decided to set up a programme for the nursery children directly concerned with the development of their confidence and self-esteem. The programme was also concerned with helping them to find creative strategies for getting support from others (Chandler, Stone and Young, 1989). We looked at what commercially produced British material was available (Eliot, M.), and also bought a lot of American material. We invited local and national child protection experts in to talk to staff and parents and to work with the nursery children and their brothers and sisters over a period of months. Over the following years we devised our own series of sessions which helped the nursery children address issues like, 'friendship', 'being safe', 'good touch and bad touch' and 'how to deal with strangers'.

These sessions were repeated every year over a ten-week period after the children had had at least a term and a half in nursery (some had had much longer). This kind of assertiveness training or self-esteem building had always been an integral part of our work, but it was now that we realised that some children needed extra encouragement to focus on their rights and to be able to set clear boundaries.

The programme created many difficulties for staff – strong, assertive nursery children are hard work but it has been much appreciated by parents. Permission is rarely refused for children to be involved in the sessions, probably because there have been hours of discussion with parents and staff before, after and during the programme. Parents also contributed to writing up the programme and their views were always respected.

In some ways the *Being strong* programme set the pattern for future parental involvement since it required a great deal of dialogue between staff and parents who were all embarking on something new and a bit daunting. It also meant that staff had to have very high levels of training beforehand and support during and after the programme; consultants (social workers with specific expertise) were brought in to make this possible. Staff also had to have time to come to terms with all their own issues about power and control, about child protection and child abuse.

1987–90 – Finding out about 'schemas'

All the staff who worked in the centre were very enthusiastic about training and staff would often give up a Saturday to be in a different part of the country finding out more about working with children and their families. After attending courses they either presented their findings verbally or gave the rest of us a written summary of what they had learnt. New staff were encouraged to share their ideas and ways of thinking; the nursery team was enriched for a time by the arrival of a music and dance specialist who was appointed to fill an additional teacher post in the nursery.

This post was later filled by a male nursery teacher who was new to teaching but who had worked briefly in Sheffield and brought with him some fascinating ideas about children's art work and introduced us to the idea of schemas (Nicholls et al., Rumpus Scheme Extra, Cleveland, January 1986; Dynamic, Vertical Schema, Sheffield Education Department, 1986). We found it all hard to understand. The language of schemas seemed so strange to us with words such as *dab, enclosure* and *trajectories* and we all felt inadequate and exposed when trying to use it for the first time. It took time for us to understand fully that the kinds of repeated patterns in children's play that we were hearing about explained so much of what we had previously seen in the way that children played but which had seemed inexplicable to us. For years after first being introduced to the idea we were filled with excitement and would search out a colleague or parent to comment on what we'd seen a child do, or share a connection that we had been able to make. As a staff group we had been looking for:

> a more conscious and articulated pedagogy which could help (us) to be aware of how to extend children's thinking with worthwhile curriculum content and how to evaluate outcomes.
> (Athey, 1990)

What we now needed was some 'conceptual cement' (Sutton-Smith, 1970).

Introducing parents to the concept of schemas

Because our agreed philosophy was to take parents with us we arranged for Chris Athey to come and speak to the staff and a group of interested parents early in 1988. It became clear during the meeting that parents were either much more open-minded than staff, or that because they hadn't got so much pedagogic baggage to unload, they were better able to listen. Their interest and understanding stemmed from many hours of direct observation of their own children; they could make even richer contributions to the meeting than the children's family workers. Parents were eager to share schemas that their children were exhibiting at home.

One mother, Jill, described how her daughter repeatedly put toothpaste all around the outside edge of her mug (edge-ordering). Ruth described how her son was hanging things from the tree in their garden, was tying ties and string together all over the house, and tying door handles and bannisters (connection); some of his play had disturbed his mother since she associated it with hanging and making nooses. Other parents described children making mounds of toys and ornaments on the sitting-room floor or under their bedclothes (envelopment); children who were obsessed with lining up toy cars or shoes. The staff could also make connections with children's behaviour they had observed in the nursery; dressing up trolleys which were transported from room to room (transporting); handbags that were found at the end of the day filled with sand (envelopment); toys hidden under things; children's need to climb on top of everything (on top); the interest children showed in getting inside the large cardboard boxes that had provided the packaging for a new fridge for our kitchen (containment).

There was a lot of energy throughout the centre for finding out more and it was difficult for staff for whom using the new language of schemas was like acquiring a foreign language. We were embarrassed and hesitant to describe what we saw with unfamiliar words and phrases, but we grew increasingly confident that we were at last understanding more about what was going on when children were playing. Many of us who had young children of our own made connections with our own self-absorbed three- and four-year-olds whose urgent need to tie the legs of the kitchen table together, or fixation with den building could now be seen in a new light. In some cases friends and family also got involved and since the head of the nursery's own child was currently in nursery she fed us with lots of information on her daughter's schemas at home and at the centre. We set up a series of training days on schemas for nursery staff, playgroup staff, parent volunteers and parents led by Tina Bruce, who had worked with Chris Athey on the Early Education Project at the Froebel Institute. These study days were enormously stimulating and have become a part of our annual in-service training since 1989.

Changes in philosophy mean changes in practice

The nursery's transformation into a workshop was now completed. Displays became a celebration of a particular child's or group of children's current schema. A spectacular working display including bicycle wheels, cogs, machinery, coffee grinders, pepper mills and a globe was a source of great interest to children who were concerned with how things rotate. Children's play became more and more elaborate and they demanded the support of staff.

Staff and parent volunteers making observations of children often had recourse to the video camera and one member of staff observed:

We now have a wonderful piece of videotape of a child, who turns the taps on full

in the nursery and persists in this activity for about half an hour despite the intervention of several adults and the interference of other children.
(Arnold, 1990)

On this occasion the member of staff who was accompanying this child's play was fairly unhappy about what was going on and attempted to set some clear 'adult' boundaries about the inappropriateness of wasting water and making a mess. Jody, the child concerned, remained unconvinced and unperturbed by this adult disapproval and continued to explore the splash, the flow and the experience of rotating the taps that had first attracted her to the sink. A more experienced member of staff then intervened and supported Jody's free-flow play, allowing her to 'wallow' in the experience (Bruce, 1991). She introduced mounds of bath mats to mop up excess water, a safer chair to stand on and offered her protection from other children with conflicting interests.

Maybe incidents like this one are memorable because they are charged with so many emotions. It takes an assertive child to stand up to an adult and demand that her right to play in her own way be respected! It is so easy for the member of staff to get caught up in power games – who's in charge; who knows best.

Challenge, extension and progression are more likely to come out of play which is central to the child's concerns. In the last chapter the story of the child who was learning by 'filling' her sieve with water was mentioned. How easy it would be for an adult to destroy that child's cognitive growth by *telling* her that what she's attempting is impossible!

Recently staff watched Peter, a two-year-old, stand in the same place where Jody had stood a few years earlier, balanced on a chair at the sink (with his facilitating family worker by his side) splashing his hands through the water repeatedly with huge sweeping movements and much laughter! This kind of first-hand experience gave Peter, who is completely blind, the chance 'to wallow in ideas, feelings and relationships [and it gave him] direct experiences through which to develop skills and competence' (Bruce, 1991). How wrong it would have been to 'cut to the bottom line' and go for skills and competence without the first-hand experience. We were, however, much more interested in what Peter was interested in; finding places in the old school hall and stair wells where his voice echoed; experiencing moving away from his family worker's arms into empty space for the very first time. We respected his courage and celebrated with him when he learnt to control his environment by establishing where things were in the nursery.

THE PARENT PROJECT 1990

Our understanding of schema was enriched at this time by working more closely with parents. One member of staff who was on a DPQS (Diploma in Post Qualifying Studies) course undertook a project which involved parents and staff in an intensive period of schema-spotting with particular children.

> *The aim of the project was to find supporting evidence that schemas exist and help children to learn.*
> (Arnold, 1990)

Staff were particularly interested in what effect schemas had on friendship between children; why some friendships were short-lived and others firm. We also wanted to explore what we perceived as the parents' richer knowledge of their children at home.

The idea of getting parents to share their observations on children wasn't new. A group of parents who helped out in the nursery had been introduced to the idea of schemas the year before and had begun talking about what they saw as their children's odd behaviour at home. They had taken photographs, collected children's work and made written observations at home. These were shared with staff who then reported back to parents on schema-spotting in the nursery through specially prepared 'schema booklets for parents'. The following extracts are taken from this schemas booklet.

> *Last year we set up a wonderful seaside area for children in the nursery. We put in this area things which we, as adults, thought were all to do with the seaside – shells, stones, buckets and spades.*

> *To our surprise some children just seemed to want to carry the sand around in saucepans and bags for days. One or two children kept putting the sand on the ironing board and ironing it.*

> *Later in the year we had a group of children who seemed to want to tie everything up, including nursery staff's legs and door handles, they also kept 'putting us in prison' by tying us to trees in the garden. We also kept finding little parcels and presents all over the place such as dough wrapped up in tissue paper and many children spent a lot of time wrapping up books.*

> *Children just seemed to want to scatter everything around, for example tip all the*

Lego on to the floor. Some of this behaviour seemed odd and some of it was just a pain in the neck.

But when an expert in children's play and learning came to talk to the staff and parents about schemas, what had been odd or irritating behaviour began to make sense.
(Mairs, 1990)

Parents were given a brief introduction to schema entitled – *So what are SCHEMAS?*:

When we began to look at and read about what children were doing with the materials in the nursery we found that they often had a pattern *in their play.*

A SCHEMA is simply a pattern *of behaviour. By observing closely what children are doing we can often identify these patterns of behaviour or schema.*

There are about thirty-six different schemas. We don't pretend to know about all thirty-six of them, but we do have some books about schemas if you want to know more.

Here are some examples of the schemas we see most often at nursery and some which parents have told us children have at home.

Parents who wanted to make observations at home were also given lots of ideas about what to look for:

Connection – joining things together

- *Are your table legs tied up with string?*

- *Does your child tie door knobs together?*

- *Has your child taken an interest in train sets, particularly in joining the carriages together?*

- *Does your child enjoy construction toys which involves joining pieces together?*
  Then his or her schema is connection.

Transporting – moving things from one place to another
The child who carries everything from one place to another and causes havoc in

your home is using a transporting schema. If you have a transporter nothing will ever be in its place.

The 'transporters' at nursery have been seen to:

- *play at being 'the council' and move all the home-corner furniture from one end of the nursery to the other;*

- *be the bus driver and take the others to the seaside (and sometimes bring them back!);*

- *load a lorry and take it to the council dump (figure 10, 10a and 10b on pages 86–7).*

Enveloping – covering or wrapping things or themselves

Does your child:
- *cover him- or herself with the flannel in the bath?*

- *wrap your 'presents' in toilet roll?*

- *wrap dolls or teddy in a blanket?*

- *walk around covered in a big bath towel 'being a ghost'?*

- *like to wear hats, scarves and dress up in your shoes?*

- *make a garage from bricks and put cars inside?*

- *fill any bags with lots of bits from around the house?*
  Then he or she is an enveloper.

Parents' observation booklets

Parents were given booklets in which to keep all their observations and a special file was set up in nursery for the project children. Parents gathered a wealth of information, and these were not all parents who found recording particularly easy.

The schemas project with parents was only one aspect of work in the nursery but in some ways it enriched all other aspects. As in the old days when we targeted children for close observation, we learnt a great deal about how children were learning and about what we were providing. We also discovered how much energy nursery parents were prepared to put into discussions about

Figure 10 (above)

Figure 10a (below)

Figure 10b

Figures 10, 10a and 10b   Alex engrossed in transporting

the nursery curriculum and the way the nursery staff were choosing to work with their children. Cath Arnold, a family worker who wrote up the project, concluded that:

- parents and staff got to know each other better;

- observers got in tune with what children were actually doing with their time;

- there was a greater awareness and understanding of behaviour;

- it was helpful in planning nursery activities in order to feed the schemas;

- the experience of a systematic approach to observation would almost certainly be helpful in the future.

REVISING THE WAY WE PLANNED OUR PROVISION, OBSERVED, RECORDED AND ASSESSED CHILDREN

What indirectly came out of the parent project (1990) was our need to change the way we planned our provision. By this time, workshop bays in the nursery had been set up to include an area for different kinds of drawing; a large area for building blocks; a home-corner; a café; an 'office'/writing area; a large non-slip surfaced area for experimenting with water (with a large sink area at child-height); an area full of materials from our waste-recycling project that children could access easily; a covered area outside, where there were pulleys, taps and water in troughs at different heights; and the garden.

Wherever possible there was 'double provision' (Bruce, 1991) so that materials could be presented in different ways which would appeal to different children and reduce the chances of children fighting over things. The emphasis was still on learning from direct experience either inside or outside the nursery. Children were also choosing to represent their feelings and ideas in many different ways in the nursery with a wide variety of media including charcoal, delicate water-colours, paint and felt-tips. When we re-stocked our nursery equipment, we concentrated on certain items like hollow blocks and wooden play blocks (purchased from Community Playthings) so that children did not have to fight over just one box if they wanted to complete a wonderful piece of construction. This also gave children a real chance to know their materials and 'become highly competent in using them' (Bruce, 1991, p. 153). We also brought steps (Gura [Ed.], 1992) so that children could climb higher as they built higher, and we talked out our own and parents' anxieties about the dangers of falling bricks or falling children.

Figures 11 and 11a   Children gaining confidence in their use of blocks

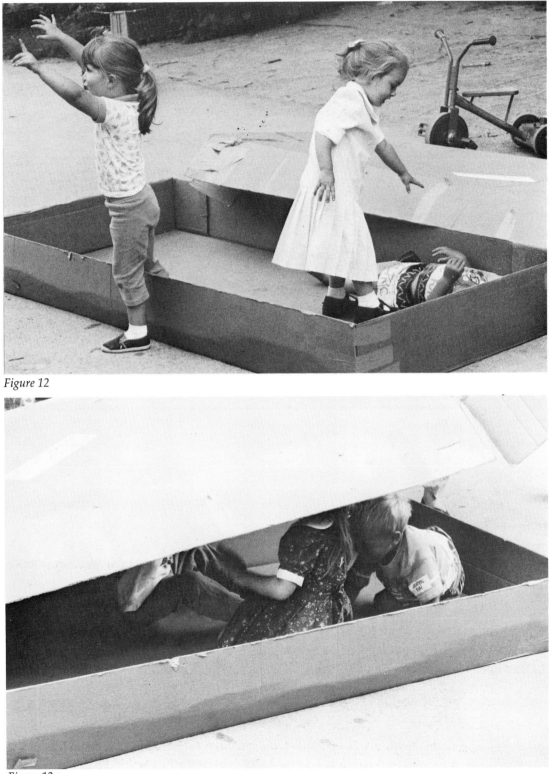

Figure 12

Figure 12a

Figure 12b

Figures 12, 12a and 12b   Cardboard boxes make a wonderful resource for children interested in enclosing

In a way, 'setting up' in the morning (which always took us at least an hour) became easier because we were not constantly looking for new materials, but encouraged children to use existing ones in a deeper way. Boxes, crates, dens, drapes, mirrors and things which worked or could be taken apart were much more in evidence than before.

We based our planning for basic provision on our direct observations of children in the nursery or on what their parents told us was going on at home (see figure 13 on page 92). We shared our observations at the beginning and the end of each day and in our staff training sessions on Monday evenings and Wednesday afternoons. We focused on particular children's 'burning interests' (Athey, 1990); the things which individual children seemed to want to investigate or explore repeatedly.

CONTINUOUS ASSESSMENT RECORD

Name of child   *Jacob K*   Date   *28/8*

Place   *Low Ceiling*   Time   *10.45*

Length of time   *5 minutes*   Alone   ✔

Group – who is in it?

How did the child get involved?   *Jacob was using the office area, cutting pieces from a ball of string. When he left the office area he went over to the low ceiling, still carrying the ball of string.*

What happened?   *Jacob was leaning on the wall of the area with the string resting on the top. Accidentally he knocked the ball of string off: it raced over the floor. Jacob raced round to pick it up. He returned to the wall. This time he dangled a piece of string, holding tightly onto the ball. He threaded the string through and then wound it back up. Calling 'Look! I've caught a fish!'*

What does the play/investigation seem to be about?

Schemas?   *Trajectory, rotation*

Links to National Curriculum Programmes of Study

English	Maths ✔	Science ✔	Technology	Geography
History	Dance	Art	Music	Drama ✔
Movement ✔				

Observed by: *Angela*

Figure 13   Continuous assessment record

As a group we would then 'brainstorm' our ideas and transfer them on to a long-term planning chart (long-term being one or a few weeks) which was known as a PLOD chart: Possible Lines of Direction chart (see figures 14 and 15 on this page and on page 94). These charts were kept in a very public place in the nursery and parents often showed an interest if their child's schema was the focus for our planning. (The term 'possible lines of direction' was first used by Wynne Harlen, 1982.)

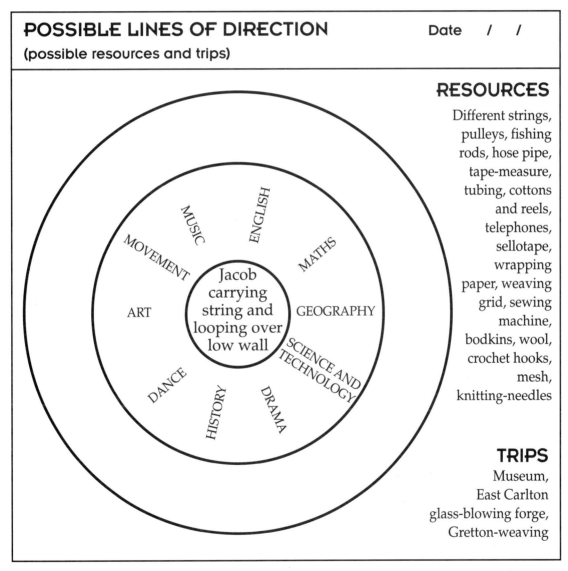

Figure 14 'Possible lines of direction' chart (PLOD) – a Pen Green planning tool for the nursery curriculum

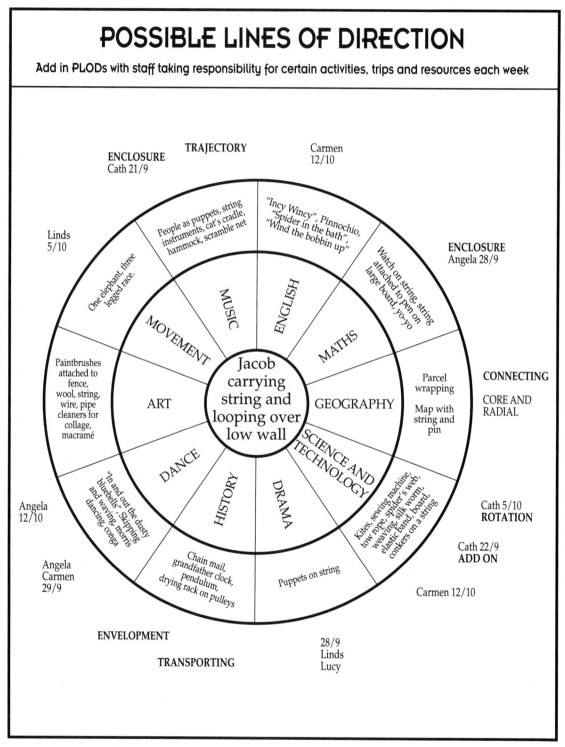

POSSIBLE LINES OF DIRECTION

Add in PLODs with staff taking responsibility for certain activities, trips and resources each week

TRAJECTORY

ENCLOSURE
Cath 21/9

Carmen
12/10

Linds
5/10

People as puppets, string instruments, cat's cradle, hammock, scramble net

"Incy Wincy", Pinnochio, "Spider in the bath", "Wind the bobbin up".

One elephant, three legged race.

Watch on string, string attached to pen on large board, yo-yo

ENCLOSURE
Angela 28/9

MUSIC

ENGLISH

MOVEMENT

MATHS

Paintbrushes attached to fence, wool, string, wire, pipe cleaners for collage, macramé

Jacob carrying string and looping over low wall

Parcel wrapping

Map with string and pin

CONNECTING

CORE AND RADIAL

ART

GEOGRAPHY

Angela
12/10

DANCE

SCIENCE AND TECHNOLOGY

"In and out the dusty bluebells", Skipping and waving, morris dancing, conga

HISTORY

DRAMA

Kites, sewing machine, tow rope, spider's web, weaving, silk worm, elastic band, board, conkers on a string

Cath 5/10
ROTATION

Angela
Carmen
29/9

Chain mail, grandfather clock, pendulum, drying rack on pulleys

Puppets on string

Cath 22/9
ADD ON

Carmen 12/10

ENVELOPMENT

TRANSPORTING

28/9
Linds
Lucy

Figure 15   A completed PLOD chart

WEEKLY PLAN – 23/11		
AREA	**PLAN**	**CHILDREN**
CORRIDOR	Add three hollow blocks Soft music Games on low table	Daniel, Zach, Nicolas Infilling Joanne, Stephen Sequencing

WET AREA	Long tray with sand and water
	Diggers and cars and container (bucket) all on floor
	Painting
	    powder
	    mixed
	    water-colours
	    liquid
		Alex Trajectory
		Chloe Infilling

WORKSHOP	Glue Sellotape	Joely, John K. On top Zoe, Natalie S.
CAFÉ	Drinks with ice cubes	Chloe Change of state
HOME-CORNER	Dried fruit and cereal	Robert, John M. Transporting Kerry Trajectory
DRAWING	Puzzles on different levels Flip chart (or easel for drawing)	James C. Tipping out Alex R. Flight
LOW CEILING AREA	Add small wooden blocks to hollow blocks and maple blocks	Daniel Infilling Zach Trajectory
WRITING	Well-resourced Letters to Santa	Chloe, Stephen C. Trajectory Alex R., Kimberley Infilling
OUTSIDE	Musical instruments suspended for targeting Sand with containers, wheelbarrows and trailers Long tray with cube and ramps Ridealongs and pulleys	Stephen C., Enzo Targeting Craig, John K., Trajectory Nicolas, John M., Stephen, John Mi. Natalie S. Transporting Craig Trajectory (Ramps)
OUTINGS	Rutland Water, Tuesday morning	Staff: Lindsey, Becky, Carrie Children: Stacy D., Michael, Keith, Steven C., Zach

Figure 16   A weekly planning sheet for planning the nursery curriculum

Generally more than one PLOD chart was kept on the go at any time since in any nursery day, a number of children would be demonstrating clearly differentiated schemas for which they wanted support. We then used a weekly planner, like the one illustrated in figure 16 on page 95 (which was again up for public-viewing), which showed how we would set up the nursery each day and where staff intended to place themselves. Further ideas were added on to this planner at the end of each day. We used coloured pens to mark what had worked well, what needed to be continued and in what way children had been involved.

Each member of staff used all this information for their own records on children in their family group, along with the observation and continuous assessment record-sheets which all staff, students and volunteers kept.

Although the structure sounds complex, it wasn't; it started with the interests of an individual child and was, therefore, fairly easy to unravel as the following account demonstrates:

> Jacob, a three-year-old currently in the nursery has, according to his parents, shown an interest in string since the age of twelve months. The nursery provision includes lots of balls of string which Jacob finds fascinating. He persists in unravelling and ravelling the string and winding it between chairs and furniture and outside among the trees. He is particularly interested in length; how far will the string stretch? He enjoys cutting different lengths of string and ties it to door handles. He is very concerned that the string must not touch the ground and is distressed when other children follow his string-tail and walk on it. What we needed to do, as a staff group, was to observe, support and extend his play (Bruce, 1991). What we did was to introduce pulleys, metre rules and measuring tapes into the provision and provide Jacob with books which would appeal to him. He particularly liked Papa Please Get the Moon for Me, (Carle, 1986), a popular children's story by Eric Carle, because the story involves a very long ladder. The pages of the book interconnect in a fascinating way and the moon changes in size as it waxes and wanes. When Jacob had explored the potential of these resources we thought about how to extend what he was doing. We made provision for moving things along the string; threading unusual things; threading metal and moving it with a magnet.

For the first time in nearly ten years' nursery planning, sessions included exhaustive discussions about the laws of physics; all staff, including our resourceful new caretaker, got involved. The PLOD charts map out how the nursery responded to Jacob's concerns (p. 94).

Celebrating the child's achievements

This new structure for observing, planning and assessing didn't evolve overnight. It has taken us more than two years to come up with something which works well for us and for parents. There is a file for each child, entitled 'A celebration of my achievements'; these belong to the family and are much used by staff, parents and children alike.

The children choose photographs for the front cover, and photographs and pieces of their work to include inside. They are asked their views on what goes on in the nursery; what they enjoy playing with and the places they like to visit. These are also put into the files. On the first home visit parents are given very 'people-friendly' observation sheets.

The impact of the National Curriculum

The time we spent evolving our system coincided with the introduction of the National Curriculum and we felt that it must be recognised in our own planning and recording of children's work. Parents and staff were once again plummeted into confusion with seemingly incomprehensible new jargon and new demands. Some staff and parents rejected the idea of the National Curriculum totally because it seemed to provide a rigid and inflexible framework which failed to start with children's interests or concerns. Other parents felt their children needed a more 'three Rs' approach and that the National Curriculum reflected their concerns. Both views have been modified in the last two years. Many parents have told us that they value enormously the time the children have in nursery for free-flow play; others still remain anxious about preparing for the later demands of the National Curriculum. A number of parents and staff travelled to see Danish and Italian provision where statutory schooling starts at six or seven years of age. They found it encouraging to visit countries where children are held in high esteem and provision for nursery-aged children is of the best quality, and where much less emphasis is placed on the early acquisition of literacy skills.

Staff now perceive the programmes of study as an *aide-mémoire* and we have reproduced sections of the National Curriculum in a more manageable form for interested parents. We know that many of our nursery children have achieved competences and can articulate their experiences at much higher levels than would be considered 'age-appropriate' by colleagues in government departments. However, our focus remains firmly on whatever the children's current concerns might be and links with the National Curriculum are made in that spirit.

Linking with primary schools

The work we undertook on planning, observing and assessing obviously had implications for our neighbouring infant and primary schools. Up until 1992 we had not sent on our completed records to the schools since they were the property of the parents. However, we welcomed staff from the schools who came into the nursery to talk to us about the nursery children. Sharing information with them was clearly important if the children's transition to 'big school' was to be a smooth one. We always devoted a lot of staff time to the children's physical and emotional transition from the nursery. The children visited their new schools on numerous occasions both with their family workers and their parents. Family workers often visited them in the first week or two of the new term to help them settle in.

What we did send on to the Infant department was a record of the children's thoughts about the nursery, about their friends and their feelings about visits to their new big schools. In this document we also included the parents' thoughts about their child's transition from nursery to school, and the family worker's views and concerns.

We have great hopes for our future relationship with local schools and believe that in future we will be able to ensure continuity with progression (Education Reform Act, 1988) in the curriculum we offer to children in the nursery and in the infant classrom. A new head has been appointed to our neighbouring school and she is very concerned that her reception staff should have time to receive information from nursery staff and parents *before* children go on to their new school in September. For the first time this year, the reception staff met their nursery intake and were shown the children's proudly-held *Celebrations of Achievement*. Joint staff training was set up this year between the primary school reception and infant teachers and the nursery family workers, with an external early-years consultant (Tina Bruce). The reception class teachers elected to use the same method of planning for children's play that we use in the nursery (PLOD) and in September the nursery children will walk into a new infant classroom which reflects and celebrates their individual interests since family workers and reception teachers have spent a lengthy session sharing the children's current schemas and central preoccupations.

THE ITALIAN INFLUENCE

At about the same time that we took on board the concept of schemas and began to make provision for children in a way that really enhanced their learning, we also made contact with nursery workers elsewhere in Europe. A number of Pen Green staff have already written about the impact of these experiences on their practice (Bebbington, 1991).

Much of what staff and parents saw supported our concern with the emotional needs of nursery children.

> *The Italian curriculum is about communication – including children's right to silence, children's self-esteem, and sense of self, and children's right to negotiate power and control within their environment.*
> (Whalley, Mairs, Chandler, 1992)

We saw some spectacular painting, designing and working with clay. Like Bruce (1991, p. 116), the Italian early-years workers clearly felt that:

> *Templates, tracing pre-structured kits, outlines like the screwed-up tissue paper syndrome, have nothing to do with rich representation.*
> (Bruce, 1991)

We felt immediately at home in nurseries where clay, wire-glass beads, and papier-mâché were readily available to children; we learnt a great deal from seeing the structures which parents and staff had designed for the youngest children, and which included convex and concave mirrors and wonderful 'cots' – types of open-weave baskets on the floor.

We also learnt about the value placed on communication between home and nursery and have since set up 'communication boxes' in our nursery where the children can leave messages or small gifts, such as a pebble or shell, for their friends. These communication boxes are becoming increasingly important to some of the children. Staff who are away or on leave sometimes send the children letters or cards which are put in their boxes.

We also came to understand that the rich environment which we offered children over two years was, in many ways, just as relevant to children under the age of two. High quality educare such as we saw in Italy could benefit even the youngest children (Calder, 1990(b); Goldschmied, 1991; Rouse, 1991). Heuristic play with babies and toddlers was not a new concept to nursery staff who had learnt a lot from Goldschmied and Hughes' video material (1987) about babies' enjoyment of each other and their pleasure in exploring the sort of natural objects which parents would have in their kitchen cupboards, tool kits or work baskets. Most of our parents seemed very aware that it was often the container rather than the present that attracted the youngest children.

The variety of natural materials used in Italy was fascinating; never had plastic toys seemed so sterile! The family room, and areas used by babies in the Pen Green Centre, have been considerably enhanced by the addition of 'treasure baskets' and we have introduced full-length mirrors into every possible location.

Figure 17

Figure 17a

Figure 17b

Figures 17, 17a and 17b   Provision for the youngest children – treasure baskets, full-length mirrors and 'ballet bars'

Nursery routines in Italy and Pen Green

We assimilated what we saw and valued in Italy into our own nursery environment. Routines were important in the Italian nurseries and they were important in ours. A parent at Pen Green, who had also worked as a supply family worker for several years, wrote of her experiences in our nursery after a visit to Italian nurseries:

> *When I thought about the children in our nursery at the moment, in particular my own family group, I immediately saw that the children who were least settled in nursery were those whose routine was upset (and/or) those children who were not getting a chance to control their lives in any way: Nicky was arriving late (at half-past ten), worried to death that she had missed lunch; Richard was being picked up early and was missing out on the quiet, controlled setting which he obviously needed to feel comfortable in nursery. Being brought together at the end of a session for stories, singing and 'a chance to have your say' was very important to Richard and I think for all the children in my group. During this year not only have we celebrated birthdays but also such milestones as Nicky being out of night-time nappies and that Jason can now swallow the tablets that he needed to control his asthma, instead of choking. We have shared good news and*

sad news about mums and dads but most importantly I feel that by giving each child a chance and space to talk, they come to know that they are special and that what they feel is important. They also realise that others have needs and that it is just as important to listen when other children are talking . . . I always try to structure the nursery session so as to incorporate:

- *welcome*
- *play*
- *snacks*
- *group time*
- *lunch*
- *goodbye.*

By adhering to routine or agreeing beforehand with the children to it being altered, for example, by a minibus outing, a trip to the snoezelen, or to the soft room, I think I have improved the quality of care I provide. The group of children I have at the moment have realised that they have a right (at least in nursery) to quality time with adults and can often be found banging on our group room door at quarter-past eleven if – God forbid – some adult has invaded their space. (Miles, personal notebook, 1992)

Patterns and boundaries within our nursery

The above account shows clearly that there are still important patterns to the day and important boundaries to be set even in nurseries like ours where children are encouraged to be decision-makers and human rights negotiators (Nicol, 1992, p. 13). Good organisation is essential if children are to feel safe to experiment. The tutor of a Brazilian student, who had spent many months researching the centre, made some insightful comments on the 'hidden curriculum' at Pen Green:

There are safety gates which the children are aware of as a barrier. I have not seen one child attempting to go out all day. There is no attempt to escape. It is a clearly marked territory. The other side of the safety-gate is the children's space, this works as an access in for children because the door is child height, rather than stopping them going out.

> *It all looks like a home! Where would you find such wallpaper in government buildings?*
>
> *The large room is not entirely children's territory. It is also adult workers' and parent workers' and parents' space. It is adult managed space which does not mean that you cannot be free, enjoy it, or move around as freely as you wish. The reason why you are safe to enjoy 'free-flow play' is precisely because this is adult-managed space.*
>
> (Colin Fletcher, 1992)

The Brazilian student herself commented on the importance of the greeting 'ceremony' at the Pen Green nursery:

> *When parents come in the mornings to bring their children one can see an important 'ceremony'. Firstly, family workers greet all parents individually and give them some time so that they can talk about their children and how they were after they left the nursery on the previous day. Or they can tell anything they wish to share with them. The family workers are there for the children and for the parents. The ceremony begins to finish as most of the children get on with their free-flow play and parents start to leave.*
>
> *This is a short, but very important contact, with parents which balances the relationship, in a 'triangle' of children, parents and family worker. It also shows how parents are valued and respected as the children's primary educators.*
>
> (Santos, 1992)

By setting-up such patterns and boundaries within their daily routine, children are offered a rich environment 'organised to enhance learning' (Athey, 1990, p. 33) in which they choose freely what interests them.

> *If a child comes into the nursery carrying a worm and they are obsessed with that worm and they want to get leaves to make a home for that little worm (envelopment), and instead the nursery worker suggests that they go and play with water or play with the sand, we are letting the child down.*
>
> (Santos, 1992, p. 57)

WHERE WE ARE NOW

The nursery was set up to be an environment where children could feel free from fear; where they were listened to; and experienced unconditional love and affection; and where boundaries were set so that children could be themselves and play within a rich and stimulating environment. Children were supported so that they could make both good choices and feel free to make mistakes. In the nursery they were treated equally, regardless of race, gender or disability, and had their many and varied cultural, religious and linguistic backgrounds respected.

The story of the nursery, however, needs to be one of those never-ending stories which young children enjoy so much. We are always working *towards* achieving our goal which is to provide the highest quality educational environment possible. We can't afford to stand still because we never quite get there.

The nursery now is a place where strong emotions are felt and expressed, and where some of the children are very angry and very sad. We want to respect their right to grieve . . . 'even though it be for the loss of a pebble' (Korczak, in Lifton 1988, p. 356) and to express their frustration and feelings of powerlessness. We also want to celebrate the excitement that some of the children are experiencing at moving from the nursery to reception classes in neighbouring schools, and to support those who are feeling more vulnerable about that transition. We have to work hard to achieve a balance between the children's need to express and understand their feelings, and their need to explore and develop their thinking.

The way we work now, supporting and extending the children's real interests and preoccupations, is very challenging to staff because the children's higher order thinking constantly takes us into uncharted waters.

The latest nursery PLOD chart had, at its centre, two children's interest in 'trapped air'. They had been exploring sheets of moulded plastic packaging which are placed in the nursery for children to walk on in bare feet and which, when pressed, make wonderful sounds. The two children's interest had quickly moved on to air trapped in a shell. Thomas wanted to put his fingers inside the shell and 'touch' the air which was making such a curious noise.

At a Monday evening staff meeting recently, we were faced with some serious cognitive challenges. We had to find appropriate curriculum content to meet these two children's interests, recognising the fact that the wonderful noises which generally accompany trapped air (whoopie cushions, balloons, bag pipes, bellows, etc.) are not very acceptable to adults and yet are a rich source of amusement to children.

The nursery in 1994 is certainly a lively place to work in and staff and children are learning all the time.

5 WORKING WITH PARENTS

A HISTORICAL PERSPECTIVE ON PARENT EDUCATION PROGRAMMES

Our concern for involving parents (principally women at first) in the nursery and family centre, like that of the community educators in the sixties, stemmed from the belief that 'education is a major determinant of lifelong opportunities' (Flynn, 1986). Community education in the sixties and seventies, however, focused on compensating for disadvantage, and often neglected the structural impact of poverty on people's lives. Views on the nature of society and social problems have changed radically in the last thirty years. Much of what they hoped to achieve in the sixties, in terms of a more egalitarian education system, has still to be achieved, and can only be achieved with appropriate political support (Commission on Social Justice, 1993).

Many of the sixties' 'intervention programmes' in England were heavily influenced by what was going on in the USA. However, most of the programmes seemed to get watered down as they crossed the Atlantic. This may have been because Educational Intervention programmes in the USA were part of a comprehensive community action programme against poverty (Singer, 1992). Riots occurred in many cities in the States in the early sixties and these (partly because of their impact on real estate values) led the United States government to search for radical solutions. Parent participation in *Headstart*, in the 1960s, has been described as part of 'the broader historical and political context of political participation of the poor . . . to ameliorate the effects of poverty' (Zigler and Valentine, 1979).

Much of the literature and research that reached English early-years community educators in the sixties and seventies put emphasis on only that part of the USA intervention programme concerned with the impact of parent education and parental involvement on children's school achievement. It ignored the political element of the programme. Little attention was paid to the key role parents had played as decision makers in planning and implementing programmes. When parent participation became fashionable in this country, the radical element in the programme was lost. There was no real shift in the power base between those taking part (parents) and those who ostensibly wanted to involve them (teachers).

Clashes in culture

It is clear from reports of both *Headstart* projects in the USA and the Educational Priority Areas in England in the sixties and seventies that many of the practitioners at that time equated poverty with cultural deprivation. In the same way 'culture' was linked with exclusively middle-class values. An example of this was the *Headstart* programme that was set up in Milwaukee with a majority of Hispanic children whose 'educational deficiencies' were attributed to the limited concepts and experience their parents brought to child-rearing. Their mothers were encouraged to take part in home-economics programmes designed to 'Americanise' them. The inference being that if Hispanic women learnt how to become American-style mothers their children's school attendance and performance would improve. In Britain, we were guilty of making some of the same assumptions (Tizard and Hughes, 1984) based on the same middle-class values. Advocates of parent education programmes always seem to require parents to make all the changes.

Women and education programmes – the need for space for development and learning

Despite the time and effort that was put into these compensatory programmes of the sixties and seventies, there appears to have been very little take-up of educational provision by working-class women. Perhaps this was because advocates of parent education failed to challenge traditional female roles and persisted in seeing women as 'appendages of home, husbands and children' (Bruce, 1986, p. 101). Compensatory programmes also failed to address the fact that for women 'individual psychological change is often needed before effective social or political change can take place', and that for psychological change to be effected, 'women-spaces' have to be developed 'in the absence of the equivalent of the local pub or football club' (Llewelyn and Osborne, 1990). At Pen Green we set up parent areas in the nursery and provided parents' rooms, drop-ins, and parent-group rooms to offer women spaces for their own learning and development. These spaces appeared to be far more accessible to them than the traditional classroom environment.

We could see from a historical perspective that neither formal adult education nor alternative adult education had much relevance to the needs of women in Corby.

In the 1970s, adult education nationally was only engaging a tiny percentage of the total adult population (Alexander Committee Report 1975) and young women were significantly under-represented. A report produced by the committee on community education at the Open University in 1976 called for adult education that was 'firmly rooted in the active life of local communities . . . readily accessible to all who need it, whatever their means or circumstances' (Venables, 1976). This was what we tried to achieve at Pen Green.

Educators missing the point

> Can people be seen as negotiators of their education instead of merely being its recipients?
> (Coburn, 1986)

Many educators in the sixties and seventies failed to appreciate both what parents were really doing with their children, and their aspirations for their children. They also failed to recognise the parents' right to an education for themselves. Parents did not necessarily want the kind of adult education that focused on re-inforcing the stereotypes of gender or class, nor the kind of adult education which focused on improving parents' 'parental skills'. Since self-confidence and a sense of control over their own lives were critical factors in learning and attainment in young children, it seemed to us that these factors were also going to be fundamental to adult learning.

How adults learn – evolving a pedagogy and practice relevant to parents

Allman (1983), writing about adult education, outlines the work of psychologists such as Piaget, Riegel and Arlin who have recognised adult cognitive development as:

> inextricably linked to the degree and quality of individuals' interactions with their social and historical contexts.
> (Allman, 1983)

The implications of their research informed our framework for adult education, particularly in relation to women who come into adult education with a very rich life experience.

'My child deserves an educated mother' – gender issues in parent education

You said 'man' and 'he'
But where were we?
Women who hold up half the sky.
You said 'man' and 'he'
But where were we?
We were invisible
We were unheard
And we know why.

(Sharon Hughes in *Reflections, Poetry by Pen Green parents grandparents and staff*, 1985)

The evolution of our community education programme at Pen Green involved finding 'ways in' to the centre for women with low self-esteem, who felt that in some way they had 'failed'. We have provided group support and group-learning environments for women for nearly ten years. It is only fairly recently that men have become involved in these activities.

The history of community and adult education, and its link with working with young children and their families, lacks specificity in relation to gender and gender issues. We were aware of the many reasons why young women become alienated from school. It was very difficult for both practical *and* psychological reasons, for women with young children to get back into school or college. Women's issues do not appear to be the same as men's issues in relation to adult education (Armstrong, 1986) and our approach to working with men in both the nursery and the family centre generally will be outlined in a separate section.

We encouraged mothers using the nursery to see the fragmentation of their lives in a positive way (Hughes and Kennedy, 1985), for instance, in terms of leaving school at fifteen or sixteen years of age, having two or three children before the age of twenty-one, and a variety of short-term jobs.

The fact that their lifestyles had been challenged and thrown into disarray by early pregnancies and enormous domestic responsibility contributed to their being very effective adult learners. Riegel (1975) points out that the most creative adult thinking 'is not that which provides immediate answers but that which first discovers the important questions and/or poses the important problems'. Most of these women had been isolated in their own homes, and they had had plenty of time to ask themselves important questions. Like

Shirley in Willy Russell's play *Shirley Valentine* they were no longer satisfied with carrying on a dialogue with the kitchen wall.

The development of an identity is a lifelong process

The twenty-year-old who was deprived of her childhood by abusive relationships and subsequent school failure, and of her teenage years by an early pregnancy, constantly has to interact with new experiences and has yet to establish a firm identity. As her adult awareness, understanding of others and self-insight grows, she can move from being controlled by 'cultural myths and the thinking of others' (Freire, 1974), towards integration or control of how she feels about herself.

Young adult women coming to adult education with this background are more ready to criticise the social framework in which they are being taught. They already have some insight into the system that effectively failed them once and are less likely to blame themselves for their failure to pass exams and to achieve. More than half the women using our community education programme in 1990 had very negative feelings about their schooling; more so than in other studies (Farnes, 1990). Typical views were: 'I am much better than they made me feel', and 'I hated school and thought that all teachers were uncaring sods and didn't like me'.

Leading learning at Pen Green

Community-based adult education, as we have come to understand it at Pen Green, requires a radically different approach from conventional adult education where the adult education tutor, as 'the one who knows', transfers knowledge to, 'the one who does not know' (Freire, 1974). What is to be taught, how it's taught, how it is assessed and who is being evaluated, are all up for negotiation with the tutor. The views and feelings of the students themselves are paramount (Brookfield, 1983).

The new role of the community educator, tutor or group leader calls for nurturing, clarifying, negotiating, facilitating and listening skills. The community educator or group leader has to be prepared to take risks, to trust the adult students and to be able to deal with their anger.

Counting the cost

Women may have had to overcome an amazing number of practical obstacles just to attend a community education group or class. One group running at the centre and testing out new Open University material listed the kind of stresses they had experienced in just getting to the group.

- Having a toddler wake you up at three-thirty in the morning and then having to stay awake and amuse her until it was time for nursery!

- Living in a refuge in cramped quarters, with no personal space and a lot of aggression.

- Having no money for the electric meter.

- Living with a partner, who was on shift work all night, with three children who had to be kept quiet when he came in at six o'clock in the morning.

The group was amused by the kind of problems listed in the learning pack which included 'problems' like parking the car!

Armstrong (1986) points out that women who want to go on to study are struggling against the tide of their own peer group, that is, other women in the community on whom they may depend for child-care and support. We have made it a priority that a free crèche is available for all groups, although finding funding for this has been an uphill struggle.

In many cases, women also find it difficult to justify the time and cost of courses to their partners. For this reason there are no charges for any of our community education groups and we have worked hard at getting sponsorships so that materials can be made available at a minimum cost. If a payment is required for a 'pack', or they are undertaking an accredited course which involves college registration, we make it possible for women to pay over several months. Again, in recent years, this has been a struggle but one that we've seen as important in terms of equal opportunities. Few women on low incomes could afford resource materials or exam fees.

We have had to address the issue of what happens to personal relationships when women grow, develop, gain new insights into their lives and their children; when they realise some of their potential and find that they have left their partners behind. This is not exclusively an issue for mothers using the centre; it also affects women staff who are encouraged to be heavily involved in courses and training. There are more opportunities now for men to be involved in courses and training within the centre, but women's commitment to their own learning still creates tensions within some families: one woman commented 'he gave me GBH of the earhole', and another woman said 'housework doesn't get done anymore, but who cares about the sodding housework'.

THE COMMUNITY EDUCATION PROGRAMME AT PEN GREEN

Current educational provision offers people 'equal opportunities' to be unequal.
(Bruce, 1986)

Many of the women using the nursery for their children started to express their need for 'something for themselves'. There seemed to be good social and psychodynamic reasons for their failure to use the route of traditional adult education. The local college was a bus-ride away and getting there was both expensive and difficult with prams and buggies; it had no crèche facilities at that time; and conventional, inflexible LEA nursery-unit hours (nine o'clock to eleven-thirty) did not coincide with college hours.

Women whose whole school experience was one of failure and rejection did not want initially to embark on more 'O' level/GCSE courses. Meanwhile, the Workers' Education Association prospectus was, at that time, offering 'O' level history, *global* politics, wildflowers and philosophy, which didn't seem to offer much to local women. What seemed to be needed was some kind of bridge for women whose lives were still circumscribed by economics and tradition and by being consistently 'other-orientated' (Carob, 1987).

Our Community Education Programme is the only part of our work which has never achieved secure funding from the local authority. The provision we offer has, however, doubled over the last decade with the help and support of both the Workers' Education Association and the local college. There was energy for change in the local community and that is what a community education programme needs to harness if it is to be effective. Through their involvement in courses at Pen Green, women in the community took action, and 'anger and frustration, consolidated and supported, is not wasted but can motivate to action' (Byrne, 1978).

Community education is in a real sense part of the war on poverty; not just material poverty, but the kind of powerlessness which leaves people feeling unable to make changes in their lives.

Staff skills for working with mature, self-governing adults

Staff at Pen Green had skills and qualifications in working with children, but few had experience in working with adults. We set up, very early on in the life of the centre, a training programme involving counselling, group work and assertiveness training. Staff spent a great deal of time together working on their own issues, their own expectations, needs and boundaries. Team building, and self-appraisal were also always given a high priority in staff development programmes.

Providing the right environment

We wanted to offer a welcoming environment to parents, recognising them as mature and self-governing adults. It seemed important to set up areas throughout the centre where there were adult furniture, adult magazines and books, cheap coffee and places where smoking was accepted.

Listening to women

Being listened to was an experience which was unusual for many of the mothers who used the centre. Some staff had roles which were primarily working with parents. Others were predominantly nursery-based. *All* staff had a commitment to offering support to adults when appropriate. Our office staff were also frequently involved in counselling training as they were on the 'front line'.

Pen Green staff shared the view that parents bringing up young children, had the right to support, personal space and self-development. We did not, however, feel that we had to uphold a traditionalist view of a 'woman's role'. Some of the staff were feminists and were aware of the 'psychological effects of social conditioning, sex roles and women's second class status' (Carob, 1987).

Moss (1990) suggests that it is often very hard for women, as mothers, to realise the kind of healthy balance in their lives that many men achieve. Many of the mothers we met experienced considerable loss of identity, depression and loneliness (Brown and Harris, 1978).

The group-work programme

Groups focus on children's needs

These groups were not based on the 'deficit model' outlined earlier in this chapter but were a response to parents' expressed anxieties over their children's behaviour and their inability to cope with the pressures of single parenthood, poverty or bringing up a child with special educational needs.

It became clear to us that while parents were concerned about their relationships with their children and wanted to address these issues, something else had to happen first. Their own confidence and self-esteem had to be raised. Some of the mothers using the group-work programme had been involved with social workers and health professionals for several years. Little attention had been given to their own emotional needs except where their psychological state clearly affected the welfare of their children. Fathers were often marginalised or excessively praised if they had made any significant contribution to the early upbringing of their child, while women were held responsible if things were not going well.

Few of the mothers using these first groups had confidence in themselves. Their own experiences of being parented were fairly mixed and some had experienced emotional or physical abuse. Most were still very dependent on their own parents for self-definition and approval. Many of the parents who used the programme most intensively felt unable to help themselves or to maintain friendships. Parents in the drop-in would stand by passively while a newcomer attempted to handle a kettle of boiling water with a baby tucked under her arm.

The women in those early parent and child groups made it clear to us that unless some of their needs as women were addressed they were either unable or unwilling to talk about 'children issues'. These parent and child groups normally involved a play session with the children, followed by a period of time for parents to discuss issues which had arisen, while the children were encouraged to withdraw and play in a crèche.

Almost without exception, parents showed a real concern for how their children were playing and learning. Some had read books on play; most had watched television programmes on child development. Some sessions went badly because parents got over-involved (a never-to-be-forgotten moment occurred when one mother got so involved with showing her little boy how to use the playdough 'correctly' that she ended the session with her foot on his stomach and the playdough in *her* hands). Sometimes parents were too emotionally confused or exhausted to be able to give their children any positive input.

It was in the second part of the session, however, that parents really came into their own. Gradually the adult 'time-out' got extended and used for discussing many issues, often not directly focused on their children's behaviour.

Groups focus on adults' needs

Groups with a 'child-centred' orientation evolved into groups which dealt with adult issues and focused on parents' needs. Unlike the continuing education groups we ran – where there was some kind of structured 'input' – these groups emphasised psychological and social development. Parents were introduced to concepts such as group dynamics, body language and interpersonal skills. We ran groups which explored family dynamics, problematic relationships and the effects of divorce on women and children.

Long-term support groups

A series of groups was set up which were concerned with supporting parents; these identified 'life issues' including bringing up children and the single parent, or having a child with special needs. Parents with special needs children had asked to be put into contact with other parents who had children with similar disabilities. A group was set up in 1983 for parents who had children with some kind of special need. This support group had educative, social and therapeutic functions. It is still running and a few of its founder members still attend.

Special needs children continue to have special needs as they grow older and their parents continually need new information and new strategies for coping with different problems (such as adolescent sexuality, or going to a new school). Sometimes the demand has been so great that there have been two special needs groups running at the same time. Group leaders needed to offer a very flexible and organic programme. At times the existence of old members has caused problems for the integration of newcomers; at times old members have been a strength and a force in the community and have achieved a great deal.

Special needs playschemes have been set up by this group. Initially they were run on an *ad hoc* basis but they are now funded by social services. Parents and children in the group go on family holidays together. Play sessions for children with Down's syndrome have also been set up and are run by parents and health visitors. Parents have visited many other schools and centres and have welcomed various professionals to the centre to discuss issues which are important to them.

Groups focus on education

One focus for group work at Pen Green was clearly educational. The centre offered an open 'community morning' session on Wednesdays which was known as a 'snobs morning' by local parents as it was the one day a week when cars were parked outside! On Wednesdays, parents, childminders and foster parents from all over the town dropped in. They were invited to fill in questionnaires about what they would like 'for themselves' on that morning.

A series of short-term ten-week educational groups on themes like 'Minder, mother and child', 'Understanding nursery education' and 'Transition to school' were offered. These were very informal but focused groups and still serve as a good introduction to community education at Pen Green for new parents and users of the centre. Parents enrolled and made a six- or ten-week commitment while their children were cared for in a crèche. For many parents it was their first experience of even an hour's separation from their child; for others such as childminders who arrived with three or four young children, it was a moment of sanity in a hectic week. Involvement in these Wednesday groups often led parents into longer term commitments to an Open University study group, or groups concerned with personal self-development.

Study groups

Open University study groups have been an important part of our community-education package at Pen Green. From the initial group studying the 'Pre-school Child' pack one night a week for more than a year, in 1983 to 1984, we have had from three to six Open University groups running every year either during the day or in the evening.

Parents have not only studied all the Open University community education packs but have also worked with the Open University course teams at Milton Keynes, appeared on film in one of the programmes, and had their voices on the tapes and their comments included in the written course materials.

For parents in those first study groups, the weekly meeting was a huge step into the unknown. Women with very negative feelings about their previous schooling found it hard at first to take time out to study. But because women felt valued in these groups, they were able to offer each other mutual support in a 'woman-friendly' environment. There was a consistently high attendance through snow, rain and even when the group leader was absent.

One of those original group members whose only positive memory of schooling was 'in the infants', now co-leads an Open University study group with a health visitor colleague, attends training in groupwork alongside staff and has completed and passed an 'O' Level Sociology course and an 'A' Level in English. For this woman, and for many who undertake Open University courses and receive a certificate of course completion, the certificate is important not in material terms but in terms of heightened self-esteem.

We realised that the course structure needed to allow for a high degree of member participation. On occasions the course material had to be set aside. Group members' personal needs or problems were considered more important than academic tasks. Most Open University courses took around nine months to complete at Pen Green, rather than the three to four months that the Open University generally recommended. This lengthy commitment did not affect the number of women attending. At the end of most academic years group members and staff visited the Open University, met course leaders and looked at new materials. They wandered around the rather atypical campus, visited the library and refectory, and experienced a higher education environment – often for the first time.

Health and self-help groups

Pen Green staff and health visitors set up a series of health-related community education groups, designed to encourage friendship and support between women, encourage community self-help, and make information on health issues available to local women.

The relaxed, caring atmosphere of a community health group gave women both the information they needed to make good decisions and the encouragement to take control of their lives. This contrasted with the traditional medical model which simply 'legitimates and endorses the status quo, and therefore acts as an agency of disguised social control' (Roberts, 1981).

In November 1983 the 'health shop' was set up; and it operated in different guises until 1991. Initially, speakers, mainly health professionals, were invited to an open group of between six to sixteen parents. These health professionals were encouraged, with varying degrees of success, to share information and take part in an open discussion with parents. Some sessions were very successful (standing room only), some were controversial and some were boycotted (either because the subject was badly handled by the visiting speaker, or because the parent who had asked for a particular session found they couldn't cope with the discussion). The health shop could respond to issues of immediate concern to families such as scares over cervical cancer, child abuse or AIDS. Sessions were set up almost immediately.

It had a huge impact on the professionals who took part. Some of them were consultants and specialists and it was the first time they had encountered a strong, cohesive and increasingly articulate group of women. The facilitators (a health visitor 'borrowed' by the centre, and a group worker at the centre) often had to support these visiting professionals who were being asked to work in a very different way. Wherever possible, parents gave feedback to the professional speakers.

As a core group which used the health shop became established, outside speakers were invited less often and the programme became more fluid and addressed the immediate, and often very personal, health education needs of the group. The group's demise after eight years was largely because health issues had become central to many other pieces of group work and needed to be handled in different ways. Individual groups were set up with a more obviously therapeutic focus such as the miscarriage and stillbirth group (again run by the centre's group-worker and a health visitor); yoga; relaxation, stress and anxiety groups; an Open University 'healthy-eating' group; a bereavement group and many others.

Assertiveness training also evolved out of the health shop. Parents had expressed many difficulties in getting past doctors' receptionists, or saying what they wanted to their GPs, so an assertiveness course was set up. On occasions, issues that came up in the health shop led on to more comprehensive programmes, such as an AIDS awareness programme, which included staff training and parent education. A session on gender issues (an unlikely topic for a conventional health education programme) gave rise to a nursery staff training programme, a policy on gender issues, and a long-term project on involving men in the nursery.

ASSESSING THE COMMUNITY EDUCATION PROGRAMME

Parents' needs and children's needs – assessing and balancing provision

Clearly, groups in a community-based family centre may not have neat and tidy beginnings and endings. They may start off as one thing and after many months or even years, staff and parents acknowledge that they have become something else. Women who chose initially to focus on issues relating to children's needs manoeuvred the sessions into groups which dealt with their needs. Perhaps parents thought that children's issues were more acceptable to us as child-care workers; perhaps as staff developed greater skills in group dynamics and group processes, we could hear what people wanted and became more accepting of parents' needs. Perhaps it was simply a question of parents building up trust and confidence as they increasingly used groups at the centre. It is clear that parents need to use the centre in their own way and in their own time.

Sometimes groups which start with children's needs encompassed parental and community concerns. In the years 1985 to 1986, there was much local concern about child sexual abuse and child protection. A young child, well known to many centre users, was abused and murdered. At about the same time the press and television gave national media coverage to these issues. Parents requested that a programme be set up to help protect children from bullying and abuse. This involved setting up an assertiveness programme for nursery-aged children which was designed to help them deal with both bullying and strangers. This programme has been reviewed and re-written and is used annually with children going to the big school. Since the programme dealt with such sensitive issues, parents were very involved at all stages. Parents made us aware that sexual abuse was an important issue in some of their lives. A group for adult survivors of sexual abuse was set up to meet the needs of adult women with life issues arising from their abuse, who also had very real concerns about protecting their children. This group has been running for more than four years, and a group for male survivors is about to be set up.

Categorising our group programme

We crudely divided the groups which we ran in the first few years into four general categories: educational groups; support groups; therapeutic groups; and health-oriented groups. In some ways this typology has ceased to be useful but the chart opposite in figure 18 illustrates the range of the Community Education Programme and uses these categories. We believe that all groups can be educative, supportive and to some degree therapeutic. Health issues now come into most groups for adults concerned with personal growth. How groups function hinges on the nature of the informal 'contract' between members and group leaders. Some groups offer 'messy play' sessions for parents and children which involve parents in supporting their children and also having time to relax and chat. Another group for parents (whose children are in the crèche) might be about *conciliation*, giving parents the chance to discuss what's best for their child and what's best for them during a difficult divorce or separation.

In the 'messy play' sessions where parents and toddlers play together, the two group leaders may have limited experience of group dynamics but will both know a lot about young children's education and development. In the conciliation group the two staff need to be much more aware of group dynamics and adult psychology, as well as understanding family dynamics and the emotional needs of children.

Getting involved: community power leads to community problem solving

Many of the groups which we run at Pen Green are concerned with psychological and social development; some are concerned with 'community power' (Warden, 1979). Often the conflicting needs of child and parents, parents and other parents, and parents and staff, have to be explored.

COMMUNITY EDUCATION PROGRAMME

Education	Supportive	Therapeutic	Health-orientated
Women returners (pm)	Childminders' group	Bereavement	Giving up smoking
Understanding nursery education	Working mothers* (pm)	Stress and anxiety management	Keep fit*
ABE next step	Family friends*	Still birth and neo-natal death	Weight watchers
ABE maths	Baby group*	Choices*	Aerobics
Women and media	Young ones*	(parent survivors of abuse)	Your body yourself
Assertiveness	Single parents*	Relationships and change	Asthma support
Theatre in education	See saw	All about Eve	Pregnancy testing and advice group (pm)
Transition to school	Special needs*	More about Eve	Massage*
Open University groups: Childhood 5–10 Health choices Living with babies and toddlers Childminding Pre-school child (pm)	Foster parents	Violence against women	Health shop*
Living with teenagers	Family group meeting	Being a parent	Health issues*
Women's studies	Parents' council* (pm)		Coping with stress*
Psychology 'O' level	Parents in nursery group*		Yoga & relaxation*
Sociology 'O' level	Caring for carers		
English 'A' level (pm)	Just a parent		
Writers' group* (pm)	Conciliation group		
Craft groups	Personal changes		
	Welfare rights		
	Tweenies/U2*		
	Mums without dads Options Images Reflections Men's Group* (pm) Playgroup staff* Save our site*		

* Group running for over one year
pm = Evening group

Figure 18   Groups within the Community Education Programme

Parents and community users were encouraged from the beginning to believe that they could change things and influence decision making from the start. That belief has never been lost. Parents were encouraged to give critical feedback, and we provided a forum which made it possible for parents to express anger and hostility.

'Parents' meeting' where parents give feedback

Assertiveness training for staff and parents made it easier for all of us to cope with conflict in a creative rather than a destructive manner. The monthly evening parents' meeting was set up to give all group members and nursery parents the chance to express their views and to plan together. Access to the group was made easier by eliminating practical problems by paying babysitting fees, giving lifts and having a very informal meeting with coffee and wine. Most recently an evening crèche is also on offer for parents unwilling or unable to find a babysitter. Minutes are kept and circulated to most parents using the centre.

These meetings have changed radically over the years. Some meetings were well attended and were purely social. Other meetings have had small numbers of parents discussing vital issues. Some parents have attended consistently for seven years, others have never used the meeting but have expressed concerns through their representatives. At times, meetings have been extremely difficult for staff, either because our practice was being criticised or, more often, because we had made a decision without proper consultation with parents. On one occasion we agreed to allow a parent with various criminal convictions to do her community service time at the centre without any consultation with parents. A large number of parents turned up to the meeting to protest. The meeting was made livelier still by the arrival of the offender who fiercely challenged the judgemental and punitive attitudes of other parents and asserted her rights as a member of the community!

Campaigning groups

Most recently, parents became very active in campaigning to save part of the Pen Green building which was under threat and certain staff posts which were vulnerable. Warden states one criterion of successful community education:

> the degree of success of political action and involvement that has been generated within the community.
> (Warden, 1979)

The 'Save our Site' group became involved in campaigning and letter writing. It attended lengthy council sessions and meetings and took part in a march on County Hall. When parents and staff did take action they were sometimes criticised for getting too involved. Since the council chambers were, however, packed with predominantly male councillors, making decisions about the lives and future of their children, it was important for families to make themselves heard.

Italian early-years colleagues in Reggio Emilio seemed much clearer about the need to be political and to be well-informed about the decision-making processes which affected their lives. Pen Green staff were visiting nurseries in Reggio Emilio during the Iraqi invasion of Kuwait and within a day there were proclamations on every nursery door which read 'Only Peace Wins' and staff were released to attend public meetings and demonstrations.

The 'Save our Site' kind of community action strongly influenced the development of the centre. Parents who were involved in this process became much more actively involved in the local community. There had been little parental involvement in local schools before 1985; ex-nursery parents are now active on all three governing bodies of local schools.

Parents evaluate the education programme

Parents are asked to evaluate the group work programme at regular intervals. Some group leaders give out review sheets at the end of each session, or at the end of each ten- or twelve-week period. Others take time to interview group members before and after they have used particular groups. Over a period of time this has given us an enormous amount of data on the nature of parent involvement in groups. We understand how and why they get involved and we use this information to help us plan new groups.

Parents also told us about how getting involved in a community education programme affected their family life. The women who agreed to be interviewed seemed to welcome this level of interest and used the interview process as a dialogue. They often came back to the appropriate member of staff with a new perspective having reflected on the questions, or having discussed them with a partner or friends.

Parent's feelings about being part of a group

I wasn't alone, I began to feel more positive about myself.

I now have others who I can speak to of my experiences and of the frustrations of life.

I feel safer.

More positive, less guilty.

More aware of my actions.

That I am important. I can make choices. I don't have to cope totally alone.

Her story – one woman briefly outlines her life history

One parent aged twenty-four, with three young children, described her situation as an abused child, and teenager.

The whole community ran from my home, my mum picked them up off the street . . . there were no boundaries . . . my childhood was horizonless.

I wasn't the sort of person who was heard . . . I didn't sleep with anyone that I wanted to until I was sixteen and twelve days . . . and it was eight o'clock . . . and it wasn't much fun!

After she had been involved in groups and courses at Pen Green for seven years she could say:

The world is what you want it to be – if I want I can make it happen.

This woman felt better able to set boundaries and deal with different situations. She had increased her understanding of how far she could fight and 'reach for them [her children]', and how much they must do for themselves. She was willing to negotiate with her own child and was able to separate her daughter's needs from her own 'she's different, she's not me!'

Using adult education as a stepping stone

For some parents their involvement in the Community Education Programme at Pen Green acted as a stepping stone for paid work in or out of the centre, or for more formal courses at the local college. For others it was important simply in terms of building up self-esteem and warding off loneliness (Filkin, 1984). It was important for us to appreciate the struggle which many women had had to make to take, what might seem like, the tiny step of joining a group. Linda Holt sums up the struggle:

Clear away the cobwebs in your mind,
Let your thoughts run wild and free.
Don't be afraid to let the tears fall,
Your whole world will not crumble.
Smile when you feel you want to,
Not because you think you should.
Don't be alarmed at the anger you feel,
Just put the feeling to good use.
Anger will not destroy your being,
So long as it is not bottled up inside,
Release the stopper on all your emotions
Show just how deep your love goes.
(Linda Holt, Writers' Group, Pen Green)

MEN AT PEN GREEN

Men have become increasingly involved in the life of the centre. In 1983, their participation was limited to dropping children off at the nursery, and occasionally attending the monthly parents' council meeting.

Setting the scene

We have tried to create an environment which is more friendly to men by taking photographs of fathers and male staff in the nursery, and having them blown up to poster size, framed and put all round the building. (For some years the centre had been decorated with posters and images offering women choices of how they viewed themselves and their role as mothers), but now we put displays of photos of men working with children alongside displays of women working in 'alternative' employment. We also bought books which were anti-sexist, encouraging boys and girls to be different and to have choices. Some fathers started to come into nursery and stopped to chat or to take part in playing with their children; but still in very small numbers.

Anti-sexist training

Women staff had had some training on gender issues and we had discussed gender issues in staff meetings and brought in outside consultants who helped us to challenge our own practice. In 1984, a colleague who had studied nursery children at home, in nursery school and at infant school shared the videos he had made with parents and staff. He showed us how much, and how early on, children adopt traditional gender roles. This led to a lot of work with parents and staff on sexual stereotyping.

Employing men and women

By 1985 we were a 'mixed gender team'. Initially, we appointed a male social worker/family worker and subsequently a male teacher in the nursery. This meant that all the staff group and parents had to find a new way of working.

> *As a staff group, before the appointment of men, the awareness of gender had been made on an abstract and theoretical level, with a strong belief in the principle that men need to be seen and experienced within the nursery and the centre as a whole. With direct and felt experience of men working in the centre, the complexities of the relationship have become clearer.*
> (Chandler, 1991)

Slow but sure change

Gradually, with increased staff awareness, some fathers began attending groups; some stayed longer in nursery and a small number got very involved in working with the nursery children. Increasingly, fathers attended family group meetings and evening meetings.

Women on the staff have continued their in-service training on gender issues. We review our practice and consider how best we can encourage men to participate in the life of the centre and particularly the nursery. We made a video on how men came into the nursery in the mornings and were greeted by women staff and learnt a lot from it. We were guilty of gender differentiation and were much more warm and physical in our approach to mothers. Recently, a member of the nursery staff has decided to study male and female nursery parents' feelings and attitudes towards 'being a parent' for a post-qualifying course (Malcolm, 1993). Nursery staff also hope to make a video on how men play with children in the nursery.

Making group work accessible to men

A variety of mixed gender groups have been run and have engaged men in small numbers. One group was called 'Relationships and change' and was run as a short-term discussion group and and then re-run the following year. On the first occasion there were three men in the group and five women. The objective of this group was to give parents the opportunity to talk about changing roles and many of the group members found it supportive. It was run in the family room as it seemed important to make the group 'available', that is, in a room where people could drop in or out. It was also fairly unstructured and was a short-term group since men seemed to find this easier.

The men's group

The men's group has met for several years (Chandler, 1993). Initially, in 1988, it was a group co-led by the nursery teacher/family worker and the social worker/family worker. It met fortnightly and focused on fairly non-controversial issues. With a change of leadership the following year the group met more regularly and began slowly and tentatively to focus on more personal issues. It has proved to be a very difficult group for nursery fathers to attend. The men who have joined have often been from outside the centre, foster carers, fathers in the community or fathers whose children have left nursery some years ago. It remains a fairly small group but has become very important to the life of the centre.

We constantly have to monitor how balanced a view we are presenting on gender issues. When the women writers' group covered a wall outside the family room with poems about male abuse and aggression, men from the men's group complained. We didn't ask the women's group to take the poetry down because the poems were a genuine expression of how some women felt. They were useful as a talking point for all of us. Instead we suggested to the men's group that they balance the poetry's message with positive images of men, using photos of the men's group week-end away in wet and beautiful Wales. One male group member wrote an honest account of the men's group's development:

> We struggled along in our early days with as few as two or three members. This in turn reflected in our conversations which to be honest were quite boring . . . The group needed a spark to bring it to life. This spark came in two different men joining the group . . . When the first new member joined our group there was no brief introduction, instead there was a very long history of the member's life, told

in a light-hearted and humorous manner. More importantly it was very intimate and personal. The whole group was enthralled by his story and its intimacy.
(John Holt, [a parent] 1992)

The same group member, when writing about the men's group in the context of the centre as a whole, made it very clear that he understood the centre's function in the community:

Pen Green is a family centre not a mother and toddler centre.

The parents in the nursery group
Fathers were not involved in this group originally but recently three fathers committed themselves to giving some time to record-keeping and observing their children at home or working as volunteers in the nursery. Two of these fathers are bringing up their children alone and the other has 'swapped' roles and his wife works full-time. One father also got involved in an NVQ study group and hopes to achieve Level II competence in Childcare and Education.

The contact and conciliation group
We recently ran a group for male and female parents who were separated, or divorced, to look at the issues of access arrangements for their children. When we ran the group some years before it was called the 'Tug of Love' group and men did not show any interest in attending. This time we positively recruited fathers who were divorced, and getting or wanting access to their children.

We ended up with five women and three men in the group. All were facing difficult situations regarding access and custody arrangement. Several were contesting custody and were very concerned over the possible outcomes.

The views of divorced women who felt it was their right to hold on to their children exclusively, were balanced by the views of men who had lost all right to access. Some men had 'won' and were finding it difficult to let their ex-wives have appropriate access. The group leaders tried with some difficulty to get the groups to focus on their *children's* rights. Group members 'brainstormed' the powerful emotions that they felt.

Guilt, anger, betrayal, pain, frustration, relief, loss, confusion, violence, aggression, love, no confidence.

Perhaps because passions within the group ran so high, the group very quickly took on a life of its own, and group members met outside group time and supported each other. The group dynamics were very different and required different kinds of skills from the female group leaders. Women in the group found expressing their emotions fairly easy; they were parents who had often used groups in the centre in the past. Whereas for the three men, being in a group was a fairly new experience; they found it hard to articulate the emotions they were clearly feeling. The group leaders had to get up, move around, and 'accompany' the anger or the grief that individual men were experiencing, by sitting close to them and giving them time.

Men working in early-years' settings

We want to continue making groups more accessible to fathers in the nursery. Paul Martin, a student from the University of Leicester School of Social Work, worked alongside nursery staff and gave us some very useful feedback.

> *When a man enters the centre, people often pounce on him as if he is someone suspicious. If a new father comes to the centre with a child, what is the reaction of the staff? Do they put off talking to him, or pass him on to a male worker? Do they feel that passing fathers on to a man is beneficial to the father, or does it make things easier for* themselves? *If the latter, why is this? Is there an issue of men talking to women staff and vice versa?*
>
> *Is it* really *important for a man to engage new dads? I think not, rather there should be men about for them to converse with if they feel safer doing so, otherwise they should be treated as a* parent *and not as a* man.
> (Paul Martin, 1993 – transcript from a staff meeting)

Paul also gave us some suggestions about how we could be more effective in encouraging fathers to become involved in meetings and groups at Pen Green.

- Staff running groups should talk to fathers in the nursery when they drop off and collect their children.

- Family workers who know the parents best, need to broach the subject of a particular group with the fathers (or their partners) directly, and then refer them on to a male worker if they want to know more.

- Fathers should be assured that the group they would be joining would be a mixed group with at least one male group leader.

- Staff should plug the fact that more men are needed to take part in the life of the centre, and that a male point of view in groups, would help this.

- Use the word 'meeting' instead of 'group' on posters advertising the groups and make sure the images on the poster are relevant to men as well as women. Keep the aims of the group general so that men can introduce their own agendas inconspicuously.

- Keep enquiring if they are available to attend and if someone doesn't turn up to the first session, find out why.

Our staff discussions about the place of men in early-years settings have been informed both by the views of male students like Paul Martin, by male staff and also by women colleagues working in settings where men form a much higher percentage of the workforce such as Denmark and Italy. Trust was an important issue in these discussions. We debated, *'Do parents, men and women, trust men to be about the centre to look after and work with their children?'* The consensus was that we *do* need to recruit more men to work in the centre, particularly men who want to work directly with children in the nursery. Our view was that *all* staff working with children should be appropriately recruited, police cleared and closely supervised irrespective of whether they are male or female. We also need to find appropriate ways of supporting men who choose to work in early-years settings, (Whalley 1993a) since they may feel particularly vulnerable both personally and professionally.

WHERE NEXT?

We constantly review our group work programme, both to evaluate what has gone before and to see what needs to happen next. The programme is driven by those who use it or who say that they wish to use it. The challenge for us now is to maintain an in-service training programme which does the following:

- enables staff who have not received any initial training in working with families to run groups and to work directly with parents;

- continues to encourage workers from other agencies to co-lead groups within the community;

- elicits additional support from what remains of the LEA's adult-education services and the colleges who are now severed from the LEA;

- continues to recognise the skills of parents as potential group leaders and invite them to take up professional training alongside staff.

Above all we have to strive to encourage equal and open access to the centre so that women and men don't feel that they have to compete with their children or each other for staff time and attention. The centre as a whole aims to be a focus for adult learning in the same way that the nursery is a focus for children's learning.

6 Staffing A Centre For Under-Fives And Families

Women finding a voice as managers, workers and parents

Services for under-fives and families are used in the main by women and children. They are staffed by women and are often managed by women, but are funded by local authorities where women are significantly under-represented at a senior management level. Women managing under-fives services and trying to do so in their own way, rather than by replicating traditional models of management, find themselves unable to access a 'women friendly' language to describe what they are doing.

The kind of words that women managing under-fives' services might use to describe their practice don't often appear in the management text books; words like *organic, celebratory, creative, forgiving, catalystic* and *nurturing*. Women in under-fives' settings often demonstrate spectacular creativity as managers. Their style is marked by an ability to balance several balls in the air at the same time; to respond to a crisis *and* maintain an intelligent conversation with a colleague; to plan for tomorrow and for months ahead while bearing in mind family constraints like half-term holidays, all with energy, enthusiasm and resourcefulness.

Women managers in early-years settings need to act as enablers and catalysts encouraging and supporting staff so that they can take personal responsibility for carrying things through and for initiating new work. This calls for the kind of leadership style which leaves people feeling that they did it themselves.

Focus on staff roles

There are enormous implications for a staff group providing the kind of services which have been outlined in the previous five chapters. It is hard to do justice to this group in a chapter or to find sufficient objectivity to analyse just *how* staff manage to do what they do so well.

Other chapters have commented on the issues of staff recruitment and appointments; the value of good, clear job descriptions; the crucial nature of the interviewing process and the need to have staff with many different kinds of experience and qualifications. The tensions that arise when staff attempt to work in a co-operative way and are line-managed through a traditional hierarchy have also been explored.

Intellectual love – Pen Green staff, parents and children are all learning

Early-Years Practitioners must dispel the myth that the precise virtue of the mother made conscious is that she doesn't have to be very clever.
(Steedman, 1988, p. 92)

Staff at Pen Green have always been: 'a bit special and a bit different' (Pugh, 1987, p. 11; Whalley, in Pugh 1992). What has been most important to the development of Pen Green as a service for under-fives and their families is that *all* the staff, however well-qualified or experienced, have wanted to go on learning. This has created a very special kind of climate in the centre.

It is no coincidence that for the last two years we have had six staff studying and writing assignments, for DPQS courses, a BTEC course in Social Care, an MA in Community Education, a CMS certificate in Management Studies, and an Open University MBA management course. Several other staff are committed to long-term training in counselling or family therapy, or they are completing Open University degrees. At the same time, staff and parents have been writing assignments for GCSE Sociology and 'A' Level English Literature and a Brazilian Masters student 'moved in' with us to complete her research on parental involvement. Parents of children in the nursery observed their children at home and filmed them in the nursery; nursery staff and nursery parents worked together to set up a new record-keeping system with an early-years consultant; and the children themselves were busy getting involved in our assertiveness programme – in other words, everyone is learning all of the time!

Valuing everyone's contribution

Pen Green staff were all surprised by the number of early-years establishments we visited where nursery nurses were still called 'girls'. Wolfe believes that 'as the proportion of women in an occupation increases its status decreases'

(Wolfe, 1978). Paradoxically this was a case of women discounting women! We grew wary of managers of day nurseries or education nursery units who referred to workers as 'my girls' or 'my staff', since the use of the possessive pronoun seemed to be a denial of staff autonomy. We felt that such attitudes reflected a belief in hierarchy rather than in a co-operative whole team approach.

Labels like nursery nurse; teacher; cleaner; and classroom assistant, lend themselves to the establishment of a pecking order which is often a denial of the real contribution of each member of staff. Our first assistant caretaker was a brilliant photographer who often accompanied children on outings and recorded their learning with memorable photographs. He also worked voluntarily with the youth club and dug and planted a conservation garden for the after-school club. The cleaner has worked voluntarily as a home visitor and sometimes acts (and is paid to do so) as a supply nursery worker. Her warmth, generosity and deep understanding of children makes her an invaluable member of the team. The cook has made the kitchen into a haven for some nursery children. In the first few years that the centre was open she also used skills and experience in physical education by working with children who wanted to use the swimming-pool at our local RNIB school.

A holistic approach to a proud profession: re-defining our roles

Staff who came to the centre with an NNEB (National Nursery Examination Board) qualification weren't seen as a homogeneous group. Some came with the experience of being parents, some had worked in a number of different early-years settings and others had exciting life experiences to share. Some experienced nursery nurses proved to be more effective at organising and taking on leadership roles and responsibilities than inexperienced probationary teachers who were unable to take responsibility for placing staff to make the nursery work effectively (Lally, 1991; Heaslip, 1987). Graduate teachers were, on the other hand, able to apply both their rigorous academic knowledge and their teaching skills, ensuring that the best possible curriculum was provided for our young learners. All the appointed staff had compassion, energy, enthusiasm and active, questioning minds.

We tried to achieve a consensus around shared values about working with children and families. We have constantly had to return to our role definitions and stated tasks, to be clear that what we *think* we are providing is what we really are providing; and whether, over time, it's still appropriate. We have chosen to call the staff family workers; family room workers; group workers and so on, in an attempt to blur boundaries between those from one particular discipline and those from another. *All* staff have responsibilities which include involvement with children and parents.

We wanted to avoid the connotations which titles like social worker, teacher, nursery nurse, or health visitor usually carry. We tried very hard to encourage all staff to see themselves as part of a 'proud profession' (Siling, 1985); one that is concerned with early-childhood education and care, family support, community health care and community education. We made it possible for all staff, whatever their core job description, to gain some skills and competence in working in other areas.

Family workers – a multi-faceted post

Working with children

The family workers are based for most of the working day in the nursery. They begin the day with coffee and a chat in the family room and then move down to set up the nursery, which takes at least forty-five minutes as there is a vast area to be covered. From about twenty past eight families begin to arrive and family workers make themselves available to greet the children in their family group and talk to parents. They spend the rest of the morning encouraging problem-solving and decision-making, facilitating, extending and protecting the children's play. Family workers are making observations and recording throughout the nursery day. At the end of the session they spend time together making sense of what they have seen so that they can meet individual children's needs on the following day. The morning session in the nursery ends with a shared family group time, during which some staff are freed to clean up the nursery for the afternoon session.

Working with parents

On a hard day, family workers find themselves constantly compromising. Their involvement in the nursery free-flow play may be interrupted by having to take time out to support a distressed parent or to work things through with an anxious child. Family workers, at moments like these, are covered by senior staff who either offer continuity to the children or support the family worker in a difficult interview with a parent. Sometimes family workers have a strong relationship with a parent experiencing pressure and opt to see that parent fairly regularly for a few weeks. On other occasions family workers encourage parents to talk to a senior member of staff with more experience and more non-contact time.

Group work

All the family workers are involved in running groups so that each has one session out of the nursery. This might involve them in setting up a play experience for parents and toddlers in another part of the building with a co-worker from another discipline. Other family workers with more experience and training in group-work, run groups which are for adults'only, such as the single parents' group or a support group for parents with special needs children. If the group work is complex and deals with difficult issues then they and their co-leader would receive supervision sessions from a senior member of staff.

All nursery family workers receive individual supervision and support at least once a month and that too has to be timetabled into their working week.

The number of people you have to be in a day

Lyndsey and Lucy, both family workers, listed the roles they took on in any one day:

friend; educator; organiser; driver; negotiator; comedienne; compromiser; manager; referee; cleaner; co-ordinator; wife; mother; daughter; team-member; decision-maker; learner; counsellor; advocate.

They also listed some of the important qualities which their job requires:

- health and energy;
- individuality;
- ability to face conflict;
- flexibility;
- open-mindedness.

The group worker

The group worker works closely with family workers in the nursery. Her or his role is primarily concerned with providing a range of interesting and diverse groups for adults. She offers a counselling service to parents and provides health advice. She also runs aromatherapy and massage sessions for babies and toddlers and supports parents concerned about their children's development, informally throughout the centre. Her role includes supporting nursery family workers who run groups for parents and she co-leads family group meetings with family workers so that they have appropriate support. This is particularly important if they are inexperienced and feel vulnerable about working with parents.

Figure 19   Parents and children enjoying an aromatherapy and massage session

Group workers at Pen Green have either had a social work or health-visiting background. Their expertise in working sensitively with adults is considerable and they have backed this up by sharing training with nursery family workers on children's emotional and intellectual development.

The family room worker

The family room worker spends most of her time in the drop-in or family room. Her role, like that of the group worker, is heavily weighted towards working with parents. She also has responsibility for setting up a stimulating environment for children (generally children under three years of age). She has to liaise closely with nursery family workers, since parents may spend extended periods of time in the family room while their children are settling into nursery. The family room worker's role involves some counselling, some group work and the setting up of an exciting and safe environment in which the youngest, most vulnerable children can play while their parents gain confidence and make friends.

Working inside and outside the centre

The family room worker encourages parents to move into activities, groups or voluntary projects within the centre and puts them in touch with specialist outside agencies like welfare rights and education welfare services. She also acts as an advocate for parents and supports them in interviews with the Housing Department, with solicitors or in court. Her role in particular, requires a sensitivity to the needs of both parent and child. Since the holders of this post have tended to come from a 'caring' background rather than an education background, they have needed additional training in working with babies and toddlers, such as the value of heuristic play and the use of treasure baskets (Goldschmied, 1991).

Administrative staff

The two administrative staff who work at the centre obviously spend much of their time in the open office and reception area. They are, however, part of the same staff network involved in supporting parents and they have a lot of direct contact with children. Currently one of the office staff is involved in co-ordinating a home-visiting scheme and works directly with a group of parent volunteers. To make this possible she has undertaken substantial training in counselling. Both office staff act as community workers. They are the first people distressed parents or children meet. The other administrative worker has had many years of experience working in family centres. She supports parents in many different ways, including co-leading a parent and baby group with a health visitor, helping parents with making DSS claims and alerting the nursery staff when parents are feeling let-down or lost.

Equal status and mutual appreciation

We give all roles the same high status. It is our experience that in many multi-disciplinary settings the roles associated exclusively with children tend to be seen as less important. Social work students who come to Pen Green often see working with adults as more 'glamorous', and certainly less exhausting than continuous involvement with large numbers of children! During their six-month placements we encourage them to spend at least one full day a week in the nursery. Some social work students have appreciated the time they spent with the children and recognised the amount they learnt on their placement about parental stress and family dynamics as well as their increased understanding of children's cognitive and emotional needs.

Family workers in the nursery were sometimes also in danger of perceiving work with adults as very complex, or too much of a challenge. They have gained enormously from running groups for children and parents. Those with more training have taken on responsibility for co-leading parent support groups. However, family workers in the nursery only ever take on one piece of group work, since most of the time they need to be available for the children in their family group. Working with adults in this way gives them a wider perspective.

Juggling roles in this way can sometimes be very demanding and stressful (Moxon, Hughes and Burgess, 1991). On the other hand, moving from one interesting piece of work to another, different but equally stimulating piece of work, which requires new skills and different areas of expertise, has meant that we have a committed staff group with at least some understanding of the pressures and constraints experienced by each of their colleagues.

Focus on staff attitudes, aims and beliefs

The women who were attracted to work at Pen Green initially came because they wanted a broader role than that which they had seen in mainstream teaching, nursery nursing or social work. Walkerdine identifies a tension in the early-years educator's role.

> There are pressures on teachers to be nice, kind and helpful, to be responsible for the provision of a facilitating environment and particularly to be the good women, putting right what some bad and pathological mother has done wrong. If children are to learn effectively they need to be encouraged to be active, creative and enquiring and in that sense there is a problematic relationship between a set of ideas about learning and the qualities desired in a teacher.
> (Walkerdine, 1985)

Our view was that staff working in early-years establishments needed to value ambivalence, and 'tolerate ambiguity and conflict' (Bettelheim, 1990; David, 1990; Watt, 1987).

A colleague in another nursery unit found that when a controversial decision was introduced at *her* staff meeting:

No-one said anything against it. It's typical of our staff meetings, how bloody nice everyone is to each other . . . we're so compromising we end up making no decisions.
(Whalley, 1992)

It is not like that at Pen Green.

Time out to reflect, negotiate and achieve consensus

We wanted to create opportunities for:

all workers to come together and jointly put forward their views about their own status, conditions and feelings, as well as consideration of the management of the group, beliefs about children and other related issues.
(David, 1990, p. 120)

The time we had together, before the centre opened, and the lively discussions and different viewpoints expressed showed us just how important it was for staff to have regular time out for reflection (in groups, in pairs or individually). We set up a variety of regular forums for staff discussion and debate by allocating three and a half hours a week to staff meetings *within* the working day. A further one and a half hours a week were set aside on a Monday evening from four-thirty to six o'clock for nursery staff to plan specifically for their work with children. (As a staff group we negotiated ten days' additional holiday on top of our normal holiday allocation to compensate for the extra time worked.) Achieving this kind of non-contact time for early-years workers felt like a major achievement in 1983; Italian nursery colleagues consider this kind of planning and study time to be the norm.

We needed to have a common understanding of staff feelings and thoughts about key issues. One way of achieving this was by staff writing down their aims and beliefs individually and then sharing them in pairs or groups until all our understanding was enriched. There was agreement that we should listen more to parents and children and not interpret their issues and values too much or too critically.

Negotiating Pen Green's rules
Rules give strong messages. We were surprised by how few prescriptive rules were really necessary. Our list included:

- deal with racism and sexism;

- deal with conflict in relationships;

- no violence, no fighting;

- make sure the environment is safe inside and out;

- no smoking in the nursery or children's play areas;

- no gossiping.

An insightful member of staff added a further point:

- One rule of this centre is that rules are not fixed and that they change, are challenged or develop.

Many staff included value statements in their lists of rules such as:

- take responsibility for yourself;

- respect others and yourself;

- don't patronise people;

- don't accept 'no' from the various bureaucracies;

- be democratic;

- listen to all;

- be interesting, challenging, different;

- confidentiality comes first.

When values are linked with standards clearly it obviates the necessity for an excessive number of rules, but staff can still disagree and this means that it's important that we provide outlets for conflict.

Bi-annual staff review sessions – using fantasy and 'emotional maps' to resolve conflict

In some of our staff review sessions we used group activities to see how people were feeling about their work and themselves and what kind of support they were getting from each other. On one never-to-be-forgotten occasion all staff (including support staff, cleaner, kitchen assistant and cook) worked with an outside consultant from a local university social work department and built a huge model which represented their fantasy of how the centre should be, using Lego, wooden bricks, 'Play People' and so on. This masterpiece took several hours to complete and staff showed each other round the sections that were their own work. Out of the fantasy which included grand pianos, jacuzzi suites and a mobile cleaning unit came some truths. Certain staff were feeling pressured or undervalued, and we arrived at some practical arrangements which could help them. We also recognised that their problem belonged to all of us.

Sometimes we used huge pieces of paper and felt-tips or finger-paints and sometimes we used another variation on the same theme borrowed from an early-years colleague (Mary Jane Drummond at the Cambridge Institute of Education). This consisted of drawing individual 'emotional maps'. Staff drew a floor plan of the building and marked on it the places they associated with creativity, stimulation or support. They also marked the places they identified as hostile, or where they experienced difficulties with particular people. Some staff found metaphors for the centre and used more artistic licence. One drew the centre as an 'enchanted tree' another drew it as a beating heart! Others were less positive and used barbed wire and dark clouds and lots of black felt-tip pen to describe their experience of role conflict, confusion or of being overwhelmed.

In the end, staff talked through what they had drawn with their colleagues and got support from the whole team for how they were feeling. They also dealt with what had previously been too uncomfortable or too difficult for them to address. This could be the antipathy between the kitchen staff and the nursery staff over who was feeling most over-worked; or between family room workers and nursery staff about not keeping each other informed. It could be an individual member of staff's resentment that their supervisor had failed to make time for their support and supervision session or had allowed it to be interrupted by telephone calls. At our last annual two-day review, we spent time analysing our philosophy statements and making sure that they were still relevant and we also studied each other's job descriptions. Staff gained a new awareness of the constraints and pressures experienced by their colleagues. Like the schools in Nias' study, which were 'not simply pleasant places in which people supported one another', Pen Green 'had also developed structures through and by which differences could be faced, frank speaking could take place and rows and arguments could happen' (Nias, Southworth and Yeoman, 1989).

Confronting issues on a regular basis

Weekly staff meetings also gave staff a more immediate chance to discuss contentious issues. They became a barometer of how included and well-informed the staff group felt. Had the senior management team fed information back effectively? Had staff been consulted appropriately? and so on. Sometimes staff energy would be so positive it felt as if anything could be achieved; people would work very co-operatively and achieve great things. On these occasions a simple twitch of the eye would be taken as an indication that someone was volunteering to pick up a new piece of work. You could find yourself hiking across the Pennine Way in order to buy a caravan for family holidays, or landed with taking a coachload of children, parents and staff to London or Leicester.

On bad days, staff would arrive late for meetings. The agenda would not have been organised, no-one would have agreed to chair the meeting and there was a marked reluctance to take on anything new. This was a good indicator that staff really were over-worked, and under pressure.

Individual supervision and support

The Department of Education and Science (1986) produced a report on combined provision for the under-fives and stated that staff working with children and their families needed to work closely with parents who might well be experiencing 'considerable stress'. They made a recommendation that staff working in this way would need appropriate 'advice and support' of a kind which was more often found within a social work setting than in educational settings.

Probably because of the multi-disciplinary nature of our staff group, we decided very early on in the life of the centre that we all needed to have regular individual supervision from someone with more experience of the areas in which we felt least competent. In this way a young family worker with fairly limited experience would be supervised and supported by a senior member of staff with a social work background and expertise in the area of child protection and family dynamics. A member of staff with a social work or a health-visiting background might be supported and supervised by a colleague with years of experience in working with troubled children and developing an exciting early-years curriculum. Parents running groups, voluntary workers, and students all needed support and supervision from an appropriate member of staff.

Although we sometimes used the terms 'support' and 'supervision' as synonymous we knew that clear boundaries needed to be set within each session so that the accountability and goal-setting element of such meetings was not blurred by the opportunity these individual sessions gave to staff to get personal support and to identify their on-going training needs. Staff began to understand that supervision was a two-way process. Both the supervisor and the supervised had a contract: to come prepared; to confront difficult issues; and to make sure that the time was shared appropriately. Family workers in the nursery also used these sessions to discuss and make plans for individual children or to receive support in preparing material for case reviews if they had children on the Child Protection Register within their family group.

Not taking things personally

This model of support and supervision means that staff have to take time out from the education and care of children, or their work with parents. We feel that they return to their direct work with families after supervision, clearer, more grounded and more positive. Support and guidance is also there when mistakes are made.

Staff learn how to deal with their emotions. If individual staff are hooked into one particular strategy for dealing with difficult situations, such as tears, anger, avoidance or blaming, then they are encouraged to get support from whichever member of the management team is best able to encourage them to experiment with different coping mechanisms. We all find it hard to get critical feedback from parents, or to be challenged by a colleague for a piece of bad practice. Supervision and support, on an individual basis, make it possible for us to hear what other people have to say about our work and to separate the personal from the professional. Adults, like children, can easily experience it as personal rejection if their opinion is rejected (David, 1990). Other staff feel that if *one* aspect of their work is not as good as it might be then *all* of their work must be suspect. The supervisory process helps staff to sort out these mixed up feelings. (See figures 20, 21, 22 on pages 142–3.)

The buck stops here

Appropriate levels of individual support and supervision are also essential for the senior staff who make up the management team. The heads of most early-years establishments do not receive adequate support. It would be impossible for senior staff at Pen Green to hear everybody else's grievances, respond to their anxieties, maintain the quality of the services and plan ahead and be accountable for the work of the centre to its external managers, if they too did

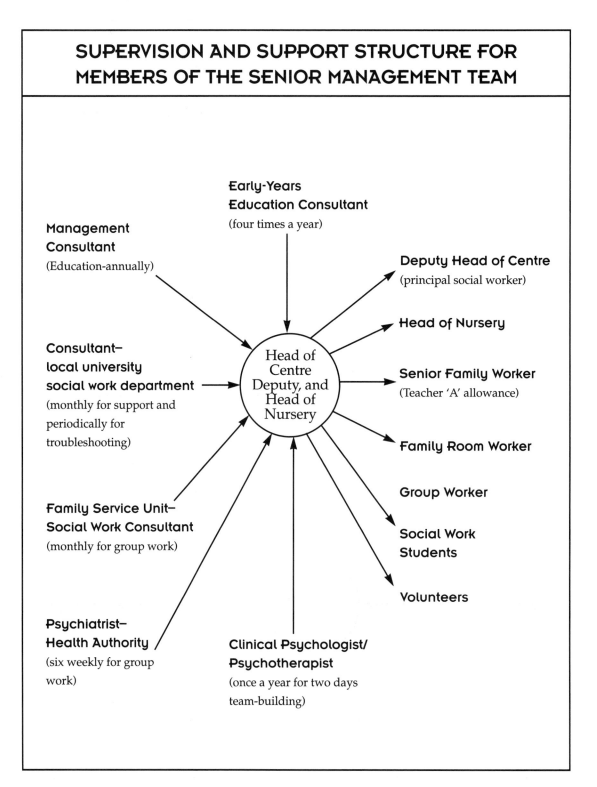

Figure 20   The supervision and support structure for the Head of Centre, Deputy Head and Head of Nursery

SUPERVISION AND SUPPORT STRUCTURE FOR THE GROUP WORKER AND FAMILY-WORKERS

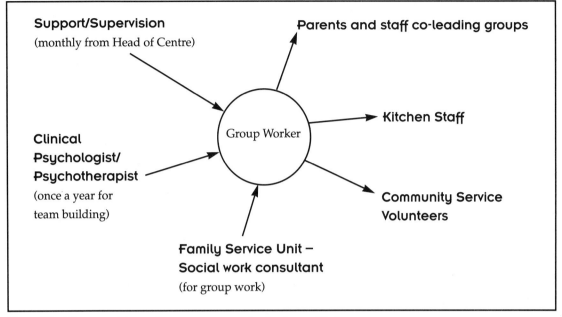

Figure 21   The supervision and support structure for the Group Worker

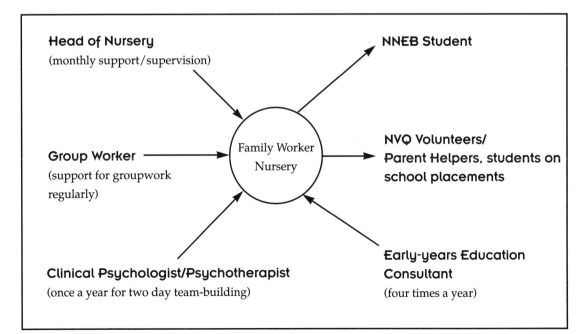

Figure 22   The supervision and support structure for the Family Worker

not get good support and supervision. Senior staff need to liaise with those inside and outside the organisation.

The management team at Pen Green have had support from a number of consultants with backgrounds in early-years education or social work. Sometimes they have felt the need for a troubleshooter to help them sort out conflicts, particularly when dealing with complex gender issues or issues around personal and professional boundaries.

Burn-out: avoiding that end-of-term feeling

The alternative to offering staff this level of support is described by Maslach and Pines (1977) in a paper on 'burn-out'. Burn-out is characterised by emotional exhaustion. The worker loses all positive feelings, sympathy or respect for her 'clients'. In early-years settings this might well be a moment when staff become disenchanted with a 'difficult' child or become angry with a parent. Staff sometimes need to be able to withdraw from direct work with people and take some time to 'ground' themselves.

STAFF TRAINING

The Education Enquiry Committee (1929) recommended very broadly based training for nursery school teachers. They felt it should include:

- studies in the history of education, including 'the place of the nursery school in the community';

- visits to nursery schools and other kinds of social and educational institutions;

- opportunities for meeting workers in other fields, for example doctors, factory inspectors and so on;

- educational tours at home and abroad.

We have to assess each individual member of staff as they join the team; help them identify their own training needs and start with the areas which were not covered in their initial teacher training. The constraints of today's teacher training syllabus, which unfortunately fails to recognise early-years learning as a specialist subject, (Curtis and Hevey, 1992) means that teachers often have limited knowledge of other agencies and limited training in working with parents (Bastiani, 1989).

Staff with training in social work may have had more experience in direct work with adults but will often have had little experience of direct work with children and no experience of curriculum planning to meet children's cognitive and emotional needs.

Our vision of training included in the first instance, visits to other centres offering similar services. We try and make sure that all staff, including administrative staff, kitchen, and support staff, get a chance to visit other centres along with parents and volunteers. They also visit places of interest in the local community and in the town centre (such as community centres, play groups, local schools and the Social Services Department).

Most staff need some basic training in counselling and group work, home-visiting, and child protection, and we provide courses either by buying in consultants or by using what's on offer from the LEA or the Social Services training section. Finding money for training was and is difficult, but we have made it a priority.

Appraising staff needs and meeting training requirements

Staff who have demonstrated a huge commitment to the centre have been able to move on because they have constantly had their training needs assessed and met. One member of staff who was very aware of her own personal and professional needs wrote the following.

> Statement of training needs and wants:
> *I'm aware that there are times in my work when I hang back, when I don't say what I'm thinking or I feel something and don't acknowledge that feeling. For example, I'll be aware of wanting to say something but somehow stop myself, or I'll feel uncomfortable, cross, sad, whatever, in a group or a meeting, and spend all my energy on putting down this feeling and not doing anything with it. What I want from training is to look at what I'm doing. How I do it. What I get from doing this and how I stop myself using my energy creatively and being more innovative in my responses. I want to take more risks and not always go for the safe option.*

A training profile for a new nursery family worker during the first one or two years might look like this.

A Training Profile

Family Worker – (Working mainly with children but also running a group for parents)
Some start with a PGCE (teacher trained) some with an NNEB qualification (NNEB trained); and experience

- visits to other centres in London, Leicester or Milton Keynes;
- visits to the local playgroup, one local school and the social services office;
- half-day with staff group on home-visiting, record-keeping, social work files, and education files;
- one day in-house course on 'introduction to counselling';
- one day course on introduction to group work;
- half day with whole staff group on family dynamics for child and family guidance;
- three day training in child protection run by Social Services centre training section and one day on listening to children;
- two away days with whole staff group looking at team-building issues;
- twilight/evening courses at Teachers' Centre on aspects of the early-years' curriculum;
- four days over the year with early-years consultant looking at schemas, schema-spotting, planning and assessment.

Group Worker – (Working mainly with adults but also linking with the nursery)
Probably starts with SRN and a Health Visitor's qualification or a Diploma in Social Work; and experience

- visits to other centres in London or region;
- visits to local play group, schools, and social services;
- spends time in nursery to get to know how we work with children (at least half a day a week and/or lunchtime supervision of the children)
- advanced group work either in-house with one of the specialists we've come to trust over nine years or at *Relate* in Rugby or the Midland School of Family Therapy Course (half day a week);
- aromatherapy training for aromatherapy work with children;
- two days with whole staff group looking at team-building issues;
- two days' course on giving supervision run by social services department;
- two days with early-years consultant learning about schemas;
- one day's training on heuristic play from colleagues in another early-years centre.

Inter-agency training

Most of our in-service training is opened up to colleagues in other agencies (as well as to parents and volunteers when appropriate). This seemed a good way of establishing some shared values and of being more sensitive to the pressures which our colleagues experience. It has been very important for us to understand the impact of legislation on other sectors and to gain some insight into how the respective bureaucracies function, that is, the Area Health Authority, the Local Authority Social Services department and the LEA.

The spin-off for our staff has been that there has been enormous 'give and take' between agencies in terms of personnel. Parents and children have benefited by being able to get the professional input they want within their own community. Social workers and health visitors are often around the centre and can be accessed easily. If health visitors or social workers are jointly leading groups or running courses in the centre then they also receive supervision from senior staff at Pen Green or outside consultants.

Training visits abroad

The staff and parents who have been able to travel to Denmark, Milan and Bologna in the last two years have gained enormously from the experience. On their return they have shared their experiences with the rest of us using videos, photos and written descriptions. Staff have since reported briefly on how their attitudes to caring for young children generally have changed as a result of seeing childcare establishments elsewhere in Europe; how their work with parents has changed and what curriculum insights they have gained as a result of their visits.

Most felt that in other parts of Europe, more value was put on processes rather than end-results and that all work with children was the result of long-term planning and deep consideration. Children were given much more respect and more personal space and time to play in quality surroundings, both indoors and outside. All the staff were surprised by the different values they came up against and felt that their own monoculturalism had been challenged. All returned eager to foster cultural awareness among the nursery children and concerned that we should be encouraging children to support each other.

On one occasion in Italy we observed a two-year-old stuck in a wooden tunnel who was very distressed, being comforted by the entire nursery group who spontaneously verbally and non-verbally petted and consoled him. We thought about our nursery children and how important it was to encourage them to care for each other.

Staff were also impressed by how much the childcare staff looked after themselves by having beautiful work environments; 'time out' for planning; good food and good coffee! They seemed to feel part of a valued profession.

However one parent from Pen Green who visited Italian provision commented:

> As a parent I want more than my child's needs met. I want my needs met.

She was hugely impressed with the resources in Italy for children but also wanted to be sure that parents' needs for personal self-development were given some kind of priority.

CONCLUSION: TEN YEARS ON

> The building was here, but we have created together the space for parents, children and staff to work, play and grow. Parents and staff have jointly defined the use of the space and constantly challenge and evaluate the centre's 'development'.
> (Pen Green Curriculum Document, 1985)

Our experience has been the kind of 'lived experience' of the area in which we work described by Bastiani (1989) and also recommended by Margaret McMillan at the beginning of this century. She insisted on teachers' colleges being built within the community and recommended that teachers should board out with the children they taught. We have come to understand the difference between inviting people to share in a finished piece of work (however beautifully tailored to their needs it might appear), and setting priorities and establishing principles together with the people who are going to use the services. Parental and family involvement was not tagged on as an after-thought nor as something that was secondary to the primary task of providing a quality nursery for children. We learnt that if we wanted real participation then we needed to share decision-making from the word go.

Family rights

Pen Green has become the kind of multi-functional early-years provision which Peter Moss describes (Moss, 1992, pp. 43–4) as having developed:

from a perspective which regards early-childhood services as a need and a right of all communities and families, and as an expression of social solidarity with children and parents.
(Moss, 1992)

We should not have to continue justifying such services (Tobin et al., 1989) but should, rather, count the cost of *not* providing them.

We took some Italian colleagues, who visited us this year, to see other children's services in our area. They were particularly excited by a wonderful local provision for children who are blind and severely handicapped, which our nursery children visit each week. They were impressed that a voluntary organisation, the Royal National Institute for the Blind (RNIB), provided so much for these most disadvantaged children. Like us they were shocked that successive governments in this country have remained ambivalent about addressing the rights of *every child*.

A community that has made itself heard

At times in the last ten years it felt as if we were taking ten paces forward only to be knocked back five paces by some new piece of legislation or by cuts to services, but we have stayed optimistic. There is energy in change and we have learnt how to harness that energy and make it work for us.

Parents, staff and children have learnt *how to be strong* and will continue to fight for services which celebrate children and honour the needs of families.

BIBLIOGRAPHY AND RECOMMENDED

READING

Abbott, P. (1987) 'Policing the family, the case of health-visiting'. Paper presented at a British Sociological Association. Medical Sociology Section Conference, September 1987.

Alexander, K.J.W. (Chair) (1975) Committee Report, *Adult Education: The Challenge of Change, Scottish Education Department*. Edinburgh: HMSO

Allman, P. (1983) 'The nature and process of adult development'. In *Education for Adults*, 1, *Adult Learning and Education* (ed.) M. Tight. London: Croom Helm.

Armstrong, H. (1986) 'Making the rungs on the ladder: women and community work training'. In *You're Learning all the Time; Women Education and Community Work (1986)* P. Flynn (et al.). Nottingham: Spokesman.

Arnold, C. (1990) 'Children who play together have similar schemas' (unpublished project submitted as part of the certificate in postqualifying studies).

Ashton-Warner, S. (1963) *Teacher*. London: Secker and Warburg.

Athey, C. (1990) *Extending Thought in Young Children: A Parent–Teacher Partnership*. London: Paul Chapman Publishing Ltd.

Atkin, J. and Bastiani, J. (1987) *Listening to Parents: An Approach to the Improvement of Home–School Relations*. London: Croom Helm.

Balaqueur, I., Mestres, J. and Penn, H. (1992) *Quality Services for Young Children*. European Commission Childcare Network.

Barclay Committee (1982) *Social Workers – Their Roles and Tasks*. National Institute of Social Work, London: Bedford Square Press.

Bartholomew, L. and Bruce, T. (1993) *Getting to Know You: A Guide to record-keeping in early childhood education and care*. Sevenoaks: Hodder & Stoughton.

Bastiani, J. (1989) *Working with Parents. A Whole School Approach*. Windsor: NFER-Nelson.

Bebbington, L. (1991) 'A direct comparison of community provisions for under-fives and their families in Emilio Romagna and Northamptonshire' (unpublished project submitted as part of a BTEC National in *Caring – social care*).

Benington, J. (1974) (p. 260) 'Strategies for change at the local level: some reflections'. In *Community Work*, D. Jones and M. Mayo. London: Routledge and Kegan Paul.

Bettelheim, B. (1990) *Recollections and Reflections*. London: Thames and Hudson.

Blackstone, T. (1973) 'The structure of nursery education: some reflections on its developments in the past and the future'. In *Education in the Early Years*. (ed.) M. Chazan. Swansea: Faculty of Education, University College.

Bone, M. (1977) *Pre-school Children and the Need for Day Care*. London: HMSO.

Bradshaw, J. (1990) *Child Poverty and Deprivation in the UK*. London: National Children's Bureau.

Brookfield, S. (1983) *Adult Learners: Adult Education and the Community*. Milton Keynes: Open University Press.

Brown, G. and Harris, T. (1978) *Social Origins of Depression*. London: Tavistock.

Bruce, A. (1986) 'Co-operative Learning with Women in Scotland', in *You're Learning All the Time: Women Education and Community Work*. P. Flynn, C. Johnson, S. Lieberman and H. Armstrong (eds). Nottingham: Atlantic Highlands Spokesman.

Bruce, T. (1987) *Early Childhood Education*. Sevenoaks: Hodder & Stoughton.

Bruce, T. (1991) *Time to Play in Early Childhood Education*. Sevenoaks: Hodder & Stoughton.

Byrne, E. (1978) *Women and Education*. London: Tavistock Publications.

Calder, P.A. (1990(a)) 'The training of nursery workers: the need for a new approach'. *Children and Society*, 4, No. 3: 23.

Calder, P.A. (1990(b)) 'Educare can advantage the under-threes'. In *Babies and Toddlers: Carers and Educators. Quality for Under-Threes*, D. Rowse (ed.). London: National Children's Bureau.

Carle, E. (1986) *Papa Please Get the Moon for Me*. Sevenoaks: Hodder & Stoughton.

Carob, A. (1987) *Working with Depressed Women: a Feminist Approach*. London: Gower.

Challis, L. (1981) 'Confusion and conspiracy in childcare and the state'. London: National Childcare Campaign.

Chandler, S. (1989), Stone, R. and Young, E. 'Learning to say no in Child Education', pp. 15–17. London: Scholastic.

Chandler, T. (1990) 'Men caring for young children: a personal account of a male worker in a child care setting'. In *Babies and Toddlers: Carers and Educators: Quality for Under-threes*, D. Rouse. London: National Children's Bureau.

Chandler, T. (1993) 'Working with fathers in family centres'. In *Changing Men and Masculinity and Caring* (provisional title) Phil Lee (ed.). London: Routledge and Kegan Paul.

Chandler, T. (1993) 'Gender Issues: An evaluation of effecting change through group work methodology'. Paper for International Seminar; European Commission Childcare Network, Ravenna 1993.

Coburn, W. (1986) *Class, Ideology and Community Education*. London: Croom Helm.

Commission on Social Justice (1993) 'The Justice Gap and Social Justice in a changing world', Institute of Public Policy Research.

Condry, G. (1986) 'Co-ordination, co-operation and control in pre-school services'. D.Phil. (unpublished) Department of Sociology, University of Surrey.

Corby Area Office Working Party Report (Dec. 1983) 'After the candle went out: A review of community social work in Corby 1979–83'.

Court, S.D.M. (Chair) (1976) *Fit for the Future* in Report of the committees on the child health services 1976. London: HMSO.

Cumberlege Nursing Review (1986) *Neighbourhood Nursing: A Focus for Care*. London: HMSO.

Curtis, A. and Hevey, D. (1992) in *Contemporary Issues in the Early Years* G. Pugh, London: Chapman.

David, T. (1990) *Under 5 – Under educated?* Milton Keynes: Open University.

Department of Education and Science (1972) 'Education: a Framework for Expansion'. London: HMSO.

Department of Education for Northern Ireland (1977) 'Well Begun'. *Theory into Practice in a Nursery School.* London: HMSO.

Department of Education and Science (1986) 'Combined provision for the under-fives: the contribution of education'. HMI Report. London: HMSO.

Department of Health (1991) 'The Children Act 1989: Guidance and Regulations, 2', *Family support, Day Care and Educational Provision for Young Children.* London HMSO.

Derman-Sparks, D. (1989) *Anti-Bias Curriculum*, National Association for the education of Young Children, Washington D.C.

Docking, J. (1990) *Primary Schools and Parents.* Sevenoaks: Hodder & Stoughton.

Dominelli, L. (1990) *Women and Community Action.* Birmingham: Venture Press.

Drummond, M.J. (1989) 'Early years education: contemporary challenges'. In *Early Childhood Education*, C.W. Desfarges (ed.). British Journal of Educational Psychology, Monograph Series No. 4.

Drummond, M.J. (1993) *Assessing children's learning.* London: David Fulton Publishers.

Drummond, M.J., Rouse, D. and Pugh, G. (1992) *Making Assessment Work.* London: National Children's Bureau.

Education Reform Act (1988). London: HMSO.

Education (Schools) Act (1992). London HMSO.

Eisenstadt, N. (1983) 'Working with Parents and the Community'. Msc Thesis, Department of Social Policy, Cranfield Institute of Technology.

Elfer, P. and Wedge, D. (1992) 'Defining, measuring and supporting quality'. In *Contemporary issues in the Early Years*, G. Pugh (ed.). London: Paul Chapman Publishing Ltd. in association with National Children's Bureau.

Eliot, M. *Kidscape including under-fives Programme for Planning and Teaching Good Sense Defence to Children.* Available from Kidscape Ltd, 82 Brook Street, London W1Y 1YG.

Estate Managers Handbook (1934) Corby: Stewarts and Lloyds Ltd.

Farnes, N. (1990) 'The Place and Influence of Community Education in People's Lives'. PhD Thesis, Cranfield Institute of Technology, Department of Social Policy.

Feynman, R.P. (1990) *What do you care what other people think? Further adventures of a curious character.* London: Unwin Hyman.

Filkin, E. (1984) (ed.) 'Women and children first'. *Home Link – A Neighbourhood Education Project.* The High/Scope Press.

Fletcher, C. (1987) 'The meaning of community in community education'. In *Community Education: an agenda for Educational Reform*, G. Allen (et al.). Milton Keynes: Open University.

Fletcher, C. and Broad, B. (1991) 'Practitioner research into social work from experiences to an agenda'. Cranfield Institute of Technology, Department of Social Policy.

Fletcher, C. (1992), in 'Nursery education in context', A.T. Santos (1992) (p. 57). Thesis (unpublished). Cranfield Institute of Technology.

Flynn, P. (et al.) (1986) (ed.) *You're Learning All the Time: Women Education and Community Work.* Nottingham: Spokesman.

Fox, Harding L. (1991) *Perspectives in Childcare Policy.* London and New York: Longman.

Freire, P. (1974) *Pedagogy of the Oppressed.* London: Penguin.

Fromm, E. (1963), in *Teacher*, S. Ashton-Warner (p. 100). London: Secker and Warburg.

Ghedini, P. (1990) Paper written for Sezione Femminile Nazionale piu partito commenista Italiano: Rome.

Ghedini, P. (1991) 'Practice and new projects in day nurseries: The situation in Italy'. In *Babies and Toddlers: Carers and Educators: Quality for Under-Threes*, D. Rouse. London: National Children's Bureau.

Gilkes, J. (1987) *Developing Nursery Education.* Milton Keynes: Oxford University Press.

Goldschmied, E. (1991) What to do with the under two's. Heuristic play. *Infants Learning*, In D. Rouse (ed.) (1990).

Goldschmied, E. Hughes, A. (1987) *Heuristic Play With Objects* [Video], London: National Children's Bureau.

Goodwin, S. (1982) 'Health visitors: help or hindrance?'. In *Supporting parents in the community*, Parenting Paper 3, G. Pugh.

Goodwin, S. (1988) 'Whither health-visiting?'. Keynote speech: Health Visitor Association Annual Study Conference.

Gura, P. (ed.) (1992) *Exploring Learning: Young People and Block Play.* London: Paul Chapman Publishing Ltd.

Haddock, L. (1981) 'Rydevale Community Nursery: a case study in national childcare campaign research papers'.

Haddow Consultative Committee (1933) *Report on Infant and Nursery Schools.* London: HMSO.

Halsey, A.H. (ed.) (1972) Education Priority, 1, *E.P.A. Problems and Policies.* London: HMSO.

Harlen, W. (1982) 'Evaluation and Assessment' in Richards, C. (ed.). *New Directions in Primary Education.* London: Falmer Press.

Hawkins, D. (February 1965) 'Messing about in science: science and children'. In *How Children Learn*, J. Holt (1967). Harmondsworth: Penguin Books Ltd.

Heaslip, P. (1985) *The Training and Roles of Nursery Staff.* Early Years Journal of TACTYC Journal 5 (No. 2) (Teachers of Advanced courses for teachers of young children).

Heaslip, P. (1987) 'Does the glass slipper fit Cinderella? Nursery teachers and their training', in *Roles, Responsibilities and Relationships in the Education of the Young Child*, M.M. Clark (ed.). Educational Review Occasional Publication No. 13, Chapter 5. Faculty of Education, University of Birmingham, Birmingham.

Hevey, D. (1982) 'The Wider Issues of Support and Planning', Parenting Papers No. 3, Supporting Parents in the Community. London: National Children's Bureau.

Holman, R. (1983) *Resourceful Friends: Skills in Community Social Work*. London: The Children's Society.

Holman, R. (1990) *Family Centres in Child Care Concern and Conflicts*. (eds) Morgan, S., Righton, P. Sevenoaks: Hodder & Stoughton in association with Open University.

Holt, J. (1967) *How Children Learn*. Harmondsworth, Middlesex: Penguin Books Ltd.

Holt, L. (1991) 'The Child Health Clinic at Pen Green: a social meeting place'. 'O' Level Sociology Assignment (unpublished).

Honig, A. (1989) 'Quality infant/toddler caregiving – are there magic recipes?' *Young Children*, 44, No. 4.

Hughes, M. (et al.) (1980) *Nurseries Now*. Harmondsworth, Middlesex: Penguin Books Ltd.

Hughes, M. and Kennedy, M. (1985) *New Futures Changing Women's Education*. London: Routledge and Kegan Paul.

Hughes, S. (1990) *'Reflections' Poetry by Pen Green Parents, Grandparents and Staff*.

Hughes, T. (1976) *Season songs*. London: Faber and Faber.

Illich, I. 'The eloquence of silence'. In *Parents and Teachers Together*, M. Stacey (1991), p. 81. Milton Keynes: Open University.

Illich, I. (et al.) (1977) *Disabling Professions*. London: Marion Boyars.

Katz, L. (1986) 'The nature of professions: Where is early childhood education?'. In *The Challenge of the Future: Professional Issues in Early-Childhood Education*, P. Heaslip (ed.). Bristol Polytechnic.

Kohl (1967) *36 Children*. Harmondsworth, Middlesex: Penguin Books Ltd.

Korczak, J. (1990), in *Recollections and Reflections*, B. Bettelheim (p. 195). London: Thames and Hudson.

Lally, M. (1991) *The Nursery Teacher in Action*. London: Paul Chapman Publishing Ltd.

Le Vine (1983), in *Pre-Schooling in Three Cultures*, Tobin, J. (et al.) (1989). New Haven and London: Yale University Press.

Lifton, B.J. (1988) *Thinking of Children*. London: Pan Books.

Llewelyn, J. and Osborne, K. (1990) *Women's Lives*. London: Routledge and Kegan Paul.

Mahler, S.M., Pine, F. and Bergman, A. (1980) *Die psychische Geburt des Menschen: Symbiose und Individuation*. Frankfurt am Main.

Mairs, K. (1990) *A schema booklet for parents*. (Obtainable from the Pen Green Centre, Corby, Northants).

Malcolm, A. (1993) 'An Early-Years Worker's Experience of the "Men as Carers Project"', International Seminar for the European Commission Childcare Network.

Martin, I. (1987) 'Community education: towards a theoretical analysis'. In *Community Education: an Agenda for Reform*, G. Allen (et al.). Milton Keynes: Open University.

Maslach, C. and Pines, A. (1977) 'Burn out syndrome in the day care setting'. *Childcare Quarterly*, 62. Berkeley: University of California.

McMillan, M. (1919) *The Camp School*. London: Allen and Unwin.

Melhuish, E.C. and Moss, P. (1991) *Day Care for Young Children, International Perspectives, Policy and Research in Five Countries*. London and New York: Routledge and Kegan Paul.

Moss, P. (1984) 'Parents' needs: Paper for women, children and child care'. Policy conference.

Moss, P. (1988) 'Services for under-fives in context: Issues and lessons for Europe'. Paper presented article N.C.B. Conference services for under-fives Development Policy and Practice, July 1988.

Moss, P. (1990) 'Work, family and the care of children. Issues of equality and responsibility'. *Children and Society*, 4, No. 2 (pp. 145–66).

Moss, P. and Melhuish, E. (1991) (eds). *Current Issues in Day Care for Young Children*. London: HMSO.

Moss, P. (1992), in *Contemporary Issues in the Early Years*, G. Pugh (ed.) (1992), (pp. 43–4). London: Paul Chapman Publishing Ltd., in association with the National Children's Bureau.

Moxon, S., Hughes, C. and Burgess, R.G. (1991) 'It's like a juggler with all the balls in the air . . . Issues of role conflict for head teachers and teachers in nursery schools and centres'. *Early years*, 11, Number 2 Spring 1991.

Moyles, J.R. (1989) *Just Playing? The Role and Status of Play in Early-Childhood Education*. Milton Keynes and Philadelphia: Oxford University Press.

Nias, J. Southworth, G. and Yeoman, R. (1989) *Staff Relationships in the Primary School*. London: Cassell Ed. Ltd.

Nicholls, R. (ed.) with Sedgwich, J., Duncan, J., Curwin, C. and McDougal, B. (1986) *Rumpus Scheme Extra*, Cleveland Teachers in Education, LEA.

Nicol, E. (1992) 'The European dimension, internationalisation education for citizenship and human rights in the early years'. *Early Years*, 12, No. 2 Spring 1992.

Nicoll, A. (1986) 'New approaches to build health care: is there a role for parents?' In *Developing a Partnership with Parents in the Child Health Services*, Partnership Papers No. 8. De'Ath, E. (ed.). London: National Children's Bureau.

Northamptonshire County Council (1976) *Provision for the under-fives in Northamptonshire*, Northamptonshire County Council.

Nutbrown, C. and David, T. (1992) 'Key issues in early childhood education' (pp. 18–21). *Early Years*, 12, No. 2 Spring 1992.

Osborn, A. and Milbank, J. (1987) *The Effects of Early Education*. Oxford: Clarendon Press.

Paley, V.G. (1981) *Wally's Stories*. Cambridge, Massachussets: Harvard University Press.

Parry, M. and Archer, H. (1974) *Pre-school Education*. London: Schools Council/Macmillan Educational.

Pascal, C. (1992) 'Advocacy, quality and the education of the young child'. *Early Years*, 13, No. 1 1992 (pp. 5–11).

Pen Green *Curriculum Document* (1985) (Obtainable from the Pen Green Centre, Corby, Northants).

Pen Green (1990) *Learning to be Strong. Developing Assertiveness with Young Children.* Cheshire: Changing Perspectives Ltd. (Obtainable from the Pen Green Centre, Corby, Northants)

Penn (1984) *Nursery Education: What Future?* London: Local Government Campaign Unit.

Penn, H. and Riley, K. (1992) *Managing Services for the Under 5's.* Essex: Longman.

Plowden (1967) Central Advisory Council for Education, Children and their Primary Schools. London: HMSO.

Pugh, G. (1987) 'Early education and day care in search of a policy'. *Journal of Education Policy,* 2, No. 4 (pp. 301–316).

Pugh, G., Aplin, G., De'Ath, E. and Moxon, M. (1987) *Partnership in Action,* 1, London: National Children's Bureau.

Pugh, G. (1988) *Services for Under-Fives: Developing a Co-ordinated Approach.* London: National Children's Bureau.

Pugh, G. (1992) (ed.) *Contemporary Issues in the Early Years.* London: Paul Chapman Publishing Ltd., in association with the National Children's Bureau.

Riegel, K.S. (1975) 'Adult life crises. A dialectic interpretation of development', in *Life-span Developmental Psychology: Normative Life Crises,* N. Datan and L.H. Ginsberg (eds.), New York: Academic Press.

Riley, D. (1983) *War in the Nursery.* London: Virago Press.

Roberts, H. (1981) *Women and Their Doctors in Doing Feminist Research.* London: Routledge and Kegan Paul.

Rouse, D. (1990) *Babies and Toddlers: Carers and Educators: Quality for Under Threes.* London: National Children's Bureau.

Rouse, D. (1991) *An Italian Experience* (unpublished). (Available for reference at the Early-Childhood Unit, National Children's Bureau, London.)

Ryan, P.J. (1986) 'The contribution of formal and informal systems of intervention to the alleviation of depression in young mothers'. *British Journal Social Work,* 16 (supp. 71–82).

Ryan, W. (1971) *Blaming the Victim.* New York: Pantheon Books.

Santos, A.T. (1992) 'Nursery education in context. A case study of a combined nursery centre in England'. M.Phil. Thesis (unpublished), Cranfield Institute of Technology.

Schiller, C. (1979) *In his Own Words* (ed. by Christopher Griffin-Beale), published by private subscription through London: ATC Black Publishing Ltd (Paperback 1984 by NAPE).

Siling, J. (1985), in 'Authority as knowledge. A problem of professionalization'. *Young Children March,* L. Katz (pp. 41–46).

Singer, E. (1992) *Childcare and the psychology of development.* London and New York: Routledge and Kegan Paul.

Siraj-Blatchford, I. (1992) 'Why understanding cultural differences is not enough', in Pugh, G. (ed.). Contemporary Issues in the Early Years. Chapman.

Sparks, I. (1985) 'Parents as managers – can the organization cope'. *Partnership Paper 7*. London: National Children's Bureau.

Stacey, M. (1991) *Parents and Teachers Together*. Milton Keynes and Philadelphia: Oxford University Press.

Steedman, C. (1988) 'The mother made conscious, the historical development of a primary school pedagogy', in *Family, School and Society*, Woodhead, M. and McGrath, A. (eds). London: Hodder & Stoughton/Open University.

Sutton-Smith (1970), in *Extending Thought in Young Children: A Parent–Teacher Partnership*, C. Athey (1990). London: Paul Chapman Publishing Ltd.

Tizard, B., Mortimore, J. and Burchell, B. (1981) *Involving Parents in Nursery and Infant Schools*. London: Grant McIntyre, Ypsilanti: High/Scope Press.

Tizard, B. and Hughes, M. (1984) *Young Children's Learning*. London: Fontana Press.

Tobin, J., Wu, D.Y.H. and Davidson, D. (1989) *Pre-school in Three Cultures*. New Haven and London: Yale University Press.

Tomlinson, J.R.G. (1986) 'The co-ordination of Services for Under fives'. *Early Years Journal of Tutors of Advanced Courses for Teachers of Young Children*, 71, Autumn 1986.

Tomlinson, J.R.G. (1991) 'Attitudes to children: Are children valued?' *Early Years*, 11, No. 2 Spring 1991.

Venables, P. (1976) (Chair) 'Report of the Committee for continuing education'. Milton Keynes: Open University.

Walkerdine, V. (1985) *Child Development and Gender. The Making of Teachers and Learners in Nursery Classrooms in Early-Childhood Education, History, Policy and Practice*. Adelman, C. (et al.). Reading: Bulmershe.

Warden, J. (1979) 'Process perspectives: Community education as process'. Charlottesville Mid-Atlantic Community Education Consortium.

Warnock Report (1978) Department of Education and Science. 'Report of the Committee of Enquiry into the education of handicapped children and young people'. London: HMSO.

Warnock, M. (1985) 'Teacher Teach Thyself'. Richard Dimbleby Lecture printed in *The Listener*, March 28th, 1985.

Watt, J. (1977) *Co-operation in Pre-school Education*. London: SSRC.

Watt, J. (1987) 'Continuity in early education, in Roles, responsibilities and relationships in the education of the young child', M. Clark (ed.) (1987). *Birmingham University Education Review No. 13*.

Welsh, J. (1980) 'Needs and resources of Pen Green area' – an unpublished report, December 1980.

Whalley, M. (1992) 'A question of choice: a study of education and day care.' (Unpublished) Dissertation as part of MA (Professional studies). University of Leicester.

Whalley, M. (1992) 'Working as a team' in Pugh, G. (ed.) *Contemporary Issues in the early years*. London: Paul Chapman Publishing Ltd.

Whalley, M., Mairs, K. and Chandler, C. (1992) 'Passion, power and pedagogy: When Pen Green met Emilio Romagna'. *VOLCUF Co-ordinate Jan 1992 Issue 27.*

Whalley, M. (1993a) 'Fathers and Childcare Services', paper for the International Seminar for European Commission Childcare Network, Ravenna, 1993.

Whalley, M. (1993b) 'Exploring the Tensions between Partnership Protection and Prevention in Early Years' Services', conference paper, National Children's Bureau.

Whalley, M. (1994) 'Young Children in Day Nurseries and Combined Centres run by the Social Services Department,' In *Working together for Young Children,* London: Routledge.

Widlake, P. (1986) *Reducing Educational Disadvantage.* Milton Keynes: Oxford University Press.

Wolfe, L.M. (1978) 'Prestige in an American university'. A paper presented at the Annual Meeting of the American Educational Research Association, Toronto, Canada.

Zigler, E. and Valentine, J. (eds) 1979. *Project Headstart. A Legacy of the War on Poverty.* New York: The Free Press/Macmillan.

INDEX